THE INTERNET GUIDE

For English Language Teachers

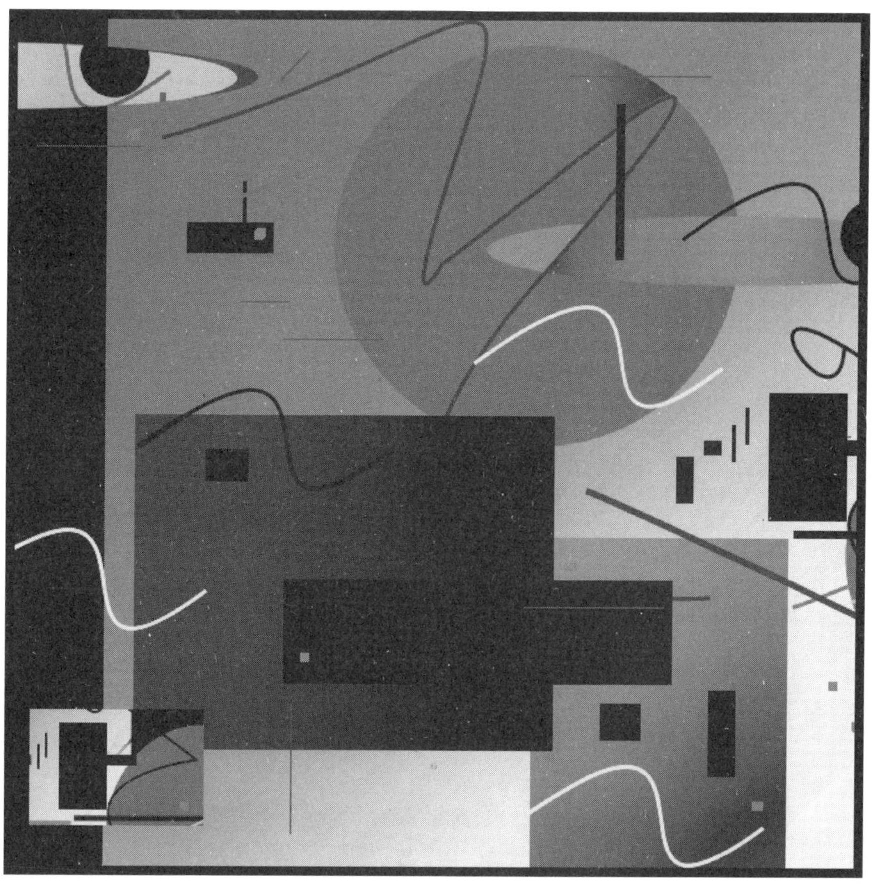

Dave Sperling

Publisher: *Mary Jane Peluso*
Editor: *Sheryl Olinsky*
Permissions Research: *Jennifer L. Hood*
Electronic Production Editor: *Nicole Cypher*
Manufacturing Manager: *Ray Keating*
Art Directors: *Wanda España, Merle Krumper*
Interior Design: *Wanda España, Merle Krumper*
Cover Design: *Wanda España*
Cover Art: *Marjory Dressler*

PERMISSIONS AND CREDITS

Netscape, p.5, Netscape Communications, the Netscape Communications logo, Netscape, and Netscape Navigator are trademarks of Netscape Corporation. Used with permission. **Microsoft**, p. 6, Screen shot reprinted with permission from Microsoft Corporation. **RealAudio**, p. 9, PN, PROGRESSIVE NETWORKS, REAL AUDIO, logos ("PN Marks"), and the RealAudio Page Splash Screen ("PN Proprietary Material") used by Progressive Networks, Inc. are the property of Progressive Networks, Inc. **Alta Vista**, p.12, DIGITAL, AltaVista, and the AltaVista logo are trademarks or service marks of Digital Equipment Corporation. Used with Permission. **Savvy Search**, p.14, Used with permission. ©1996 Daniel Dreilinger. **ESL Search Page**, p.14, Used with Permission. **Magellan**, p.15, Used with permission of the McKinley Group. **YAHOO**, p.16, Text and artwork ©1996 by YAHOO!, Inc. All rights reserved. YAHOO! and the YAHOO! logo are trademarks of Yahoo!, Inc. **ERIC,** p.17, Used with permission of ERIC Clearinghouse on Assessment and Evaluation. **Bigfoot**, p.18, Used with permission of Bigfoot Partners, L.P. **CELIA**, p.21, Used with permission. **Virtual CALL Library**, p.22, Used with permission. **Cu-SeeMe**, p.41, Used with permission of White Pine Software. **Grammar Safari,** p.66, Text and logo by Douglas Mills and Ann Salzmann, Intensive English Institute and Division of English as an International Language. University of Illinois at Urbana-Champaign. ©1995 The Board of Trustees of the University of Illinois. All rights reserved. **On-line English Grammar**, p.66, Used with permission of Digital Education Network Ltd. **The Electric Newstand**, p.73, Used with permission of the Electronic Newstand, the Ultimate Magazine Site. **Tongue Twister Database**, p.92, ©1996 C.T. Staley. **American Slanguages**, p.94, Used with permission of Mike Ellis, author and Creator of Slanguage (mike1@slanguage.com). **ESL Random Idiom Page**, p.95 Used with permission. **Merriam-Webster's Word of the Day**, p.96, Used with permission. ©1996 by Merriam-Webster Inc., publisher of Merriam-Webster dictionaries and reference books. **The Graffiti Wall**, p.97, Used with permission. **Purdue On-Line Writing Lab**, p. 98, Used with permission of the Purdue Research Foundation.

Prentice-Hall, Inc.
A Simon & Schuster Company
Upper Saddle River, New Jersey 07458

Printed in the United States of America

10 9 8 7 6 5 4

ISBN 0-13-841073-9

Prentice-Hall International (UK) Limited, *London*
Prentice-Hall of Australia Pty. Limited, *Sydney*
Prentice-Hall Canada Inc., *Toronto*
Prentice-Hall Hispanoamericana, S.A., *Mexico*
Prentice-Hall of India Private Limited, *New Delhi*
Prentice-Hall of Japan, Inc., *Tokyo*
Simon & Schuster Asia Pte. Ltd., *Singapore*
Editora Prentice-Hall do Brasil, Ltda., *Rio de Janeiro*

Contents

For Benjamin,
who wants to be a teacher like his Daddy.

Acknowledgments

I would like to thank:

Dao and Benjamin,
for their love and patience.

Sheryl Olinsky,
for without her this book would not exist.

Dennis Oliver,
for his continuous support and encouragement.

Jennifer Hood,
for being a true "permissions guru"

Patty Clark,
for her courage and optimism under extreme adversity.

Daniele Dibie and the ESL staff and students at California State University, Northridge,
for their help and understanding.

Roy Bowers, Lauren Rosen, and Spencer Schneider,
for their ingenuity on how to use the Internet in an ESL/EFL classroom.

And to the many individuals from TESL-L, Neteach-L, and the ESL Cafe,
for their excellent feedback, suggestions, and support.

Introduction

My love affair with the Internet began back in 1992 when, with my trusty Mac and a very slow modem, I managed to send my first e-mail message from my house in Los Angeles, all the way to a friend across the world in Thailand. And when I received a message back from him in a matter of minutes, you can't even imagine my exhilaration!

Four years later, to my astonishment, I'm still excited. In this book I'll try my best to share with you some of my enthusiasm by showing you how to :

- **Navigate the World Wide Web**
- **Send electronic mail**
- **Find the information you're looking for**
- **Locate and download software**
- **Meet and communicate with people from around the world**
- **Use the Internet in your teaching**
- **Create and promote your very own Web page**
- **Even find a job**

And if that's not enough, I'll also share with you several hundred of my favorite ESL/EFL Web sites, gathered from my voluminous journeys (and several hundred hours) across the World Wide Web.

Remember: Things Change

I've tried my best to keep everything as up-to-date and accurate as possible, but the Internet is a dynamic entity where things are continuously evolving—addresses change, sites close down, technology becomes outdated, and products come and go. If you have any problems, spot any errors, or just feel like saying hello, please feel free to e-mail me at:

`sperling@eslcafe.com`

In addition, I'll be keeping things current on my Update Page located at:

`http://www.eslcafe.com/book/`

You'll also find a bulletin board where you can give me instant feedback for future editions of this book. It's located at:

`http://www.eslcafe.com/book/wwwboard.html`

I'd love to hear from you!

Dave Sperling
California State University, Northridge
March 10, 1997

Welcome to the Internet!

“The Internet to me is like a library which is five minutes old. People who say they can find things quicker with a stroll to the local library are missing the point. The Net is young—one day it will be complete. It’s a vibrant place, particularly with regard to ESL/EFL teachers and what they are doing. Also a great place for those of us who need access to ‘pop culture’ information for our students.”

Gavin Dudeney
International House, Barcelona, Spain
dudeney@encomix.es

The Internet: What’s in It for Me?

Everyone (and I mean everyone!) seems to be getting onto the Internet on-ramp these days, but what exactly is this so called “Information Superhighway?” That’s not an easy question to answer but try visualizing it as a magnificent global network with millions and millions of computers (and, of course, people) connected to one another, where each day people throughout the world exchange an immeasurable amount of information, electronic mail, news, pictures, resources, and, more importantly, ideas.

But how does all this help you and your class? Well, imagine an infinite number of resources available for your students to improve their skills in reading, writing, grammar, listening, pronunciation, vocabulary, idioms, slang, Test of English as a Foreign Language, and even conversation. Or contemplate your class sharing their creativity with the entire world—essays, poems, recipes, biographies, or even art work. Or perhaps communicating—with text, voice, and live video—with ESL/EFL classes from all parts of the world. Astounding, isn’t it?

And what’s in it for you, the teacher? Well, you’ll find the Internet to be an exhilarating tool for meeting and brainstorming with other teachers and students from around the world, locating and gathering class material, reading the latest journal articles and publications, accessing language learning software, and even finding a new teaching job. Sounds wonderful, doesn’t it? It is!

A Brief History of the Internet

The history of the Internet dates back to 1969, when the Defense Advanced Research Projects Agency decided to create a way for computers to "talk" to one another over standard telephone lines. Their network of computers was called DARPANET (soon to become known as ARPANET), which quickly grew as more and more computers became a part of this expanding network.

The idea of a network soon became a popular means for scientists and researchers to communicate and share ideas with one another. In 1984 the National Science Foundation started the NSFNET network, which linked five supercomputer centers. Universities were then able to easily enter this network by accessing one of the five supercomputer centers.

NSFNET grew rapidly, as every school and government agency wanted to become part of this exciting international network. As more and more computers became interconnected, NSFNET became known as the ***Inter-Net-Network***, otherwise known as the **Internet**. Today there are millions of computers from nearly every country in the world connected to the Internet, and many more millions of Internet users.

Internet 101: The Basics

A lot of people think that the Internet is just a single entity, but the truth is that the Internet is made up of a combination of various software applications, each with their own unique function. Once on the **Net** (as the Internet is often called), you'll be able to enjoy such goodies as:

- **E-mail** — Electronic mail allows you to instantly send and receive messages from around the world.
- **World Wide Web** — With its colorful mix of hyperlinks, text, graphics, images, sound, and video, the **Web** is where it's at!
- **Gopher** — Another way of exploring the Internet to find information.
- **File Transfer Protocol (FTP)** — A way to transfer files from one computer to another computer over the Internet.
- **Telnet** — An application that enables you to log in to another computer system on the Internet.
- **USENET Newsgroups** — A network of more than 20,000 discussion groups on thousands of specialized topics.
- **Chat** — A way to communicate in real time with other users whereby those users type simultaneously.
- **Audio** — Communicating as with a telephone over the Internet.
- **Videoconferencing** — Voice and video communication.
- **And More!**

Getting Connected

Now that I've got you all excited about what the Internet's all about, let's learn a little bit about how to get you and your class up and running. Here's what you need:

- **A computer** Of course you'll need a computer in order to hook up to the Net, and almost any one will do. However, in order to take advantage of the latest and greatest Internet software (like **Netscape Navigator** for exploring the Web), you'll need a late-model Macintosh or a PC running Microsoft Windows or Windows 95. Lots of memory (RAM) helps, too.
- **A modem** It's the modem that enables your computer to transfer data over the phone lines and therefore connect you to the Internet. Modems come in various speeds measured in **bps**, or **bits per second**. Do yourself a favor, however, and buy the fastest modem possible (I suggest 28,800 or 33,600 bps) because it will make your journey a lot more pleasant.

Types of Connections

Dial-up Accounts

Now that your computer and modem are set up, you'll need an Internet connection. The most common type is through a **Dial-up** account, where you dial into your Internet account through your modem. There are three types of dial-up accounts:

1. **Terminal Connection** Also called a **shell account**, this is the most basic type of Internet access, giving you a text-only environment with little or no **graphics** (images and pictures). Use only as a last resort!
2. **SLIP/PPP Connection** Slip (Serial Line Interface Protocol) and PPP (Point-to-Point Protocol) are quickly becoming the most common way for people at home to access the Internet. This type of connection enables you to directly connect to the Internet via an Internet Service Provider (**ISP**), enabling you to use the newest and best graphical Internet software.

Tip: For the world's most comprehensive and up-to-date listing of Internet Service Providers, surf over to *The List* **`(http://thelist.iworld.com/)`**, where you can search a database of thousands of ISPs from around the world.

3. **Commercial Online Access** Millions of users have Internet access through large commercial online companies, which usually simplify the process of installing and configuring Internet software, as well as provide access to their own services and forums. Remember, however, that you might be limited to using only their Internet software (which is not always good), and the cost is also often more expensive than local or national Internet Service Providers. You'll find that it pays to shop around.

The four online giants are:

America Online
(800) 827-6364
(http://www.aol.com/)
$19.95 a month for unlimited access.

CompuServe
(800) 848-8199
(http://www.compuserve.com/)
$9.95 a month for 5 hours, $2.95 for each additional hour; $24.95 a month for 20 hours, $1.95 for each additional hour.

Prodigy
(800) 776-3449
(http://www.prodigy.com/)
$19.95 a month for unlimited access.

Microsoft Network (MSN)
(800) 386-5550
(http://www.msn.com)
$19.95 a month for unlimited access.

Dedicated Connections

Most colleges, universities, and schools offer a high-speed dedicated connection, where the computers on campus are permanently connected to the Internet. This type of connection is fast, doesn't require a modem to dial, and is always linked to the Internet, 24 hours a day.

A Peek into the Future

There's no doubt that the Internet will become increasingly faster, with graphics, sound, and video images instantly flashing across the screen. **ISDN** (Integrated Services Digital Network) is already available in many places, and offers a high-speed digital telephone connection to the Internet, with speeds of 56,000 to 128,000 bps (and that's fast!). At this time, however, ISDN is still expensive in many areas, so call your local telephone company for more information.

Also keep an eye out for satellite connections, with speeds hovering around 182,000 bps, and cable modems,with lightning speeds starting at a whopping 500,000 bps!

The World Wide Web

The World Wide Web (also called **WWW**, or the **Web**), is fast becoming the most popular area of the Internet. With its mix of text and multimedia—and user-friendliness thrown in—the Web is a magnificent collection of interconnected documents (called Web pages) from around the globe.

The Web began in Switzerland at CERN (The European Laboratory for Particle Physics), where scientists developed **hypertext**, an easier method of navigating the Internet, where text is used to link documents. With hypertext, a simple click of the mouse enables you to easily jump around the world: to read the latest news in *The New York Times*, search for teaching material in Australia, chat with friends in South Africa, view paintings from art galleries in Paris, listen to pop music from Korea, download the newest software in California, and even participate in live videoconferencing with an ESL/EFL class in another country.

Web Browsers

To access the Web, you'll need a **Web browser**, which is the software through which you navigate the World Wide Web. There are lots of Web browsers on the market, but the two most popular are **Netscape Navigator** and **Microsoft Explorer**.

Netscape Navigator
(http://home.netscape.com/)
My personal favorite, it's powerful, easy to use, and performs equally well on the Mac, Windows, and UNIX.

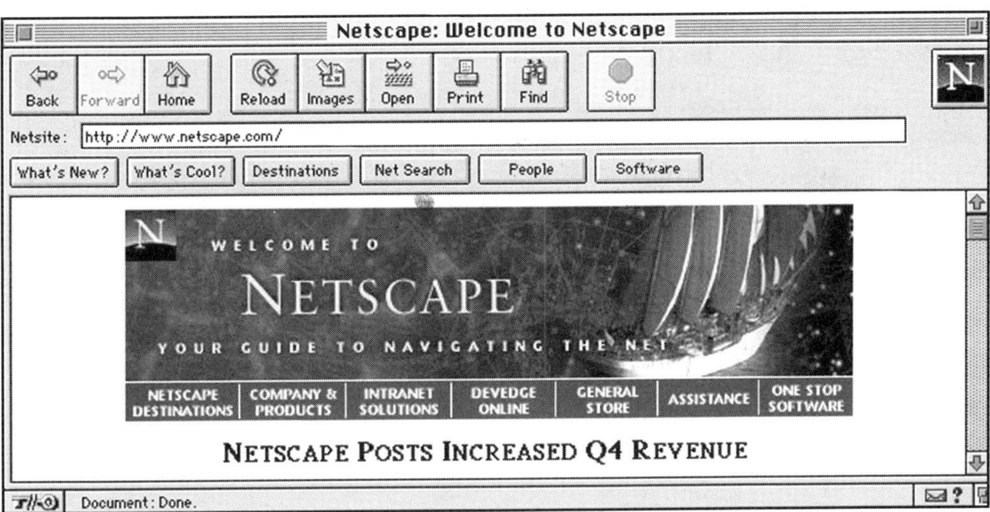

Microsoft Explorer
`(http://microsoft.com/)`
Also very easy to use. It does have an advantage, however, over most of the competition: all versions are free.

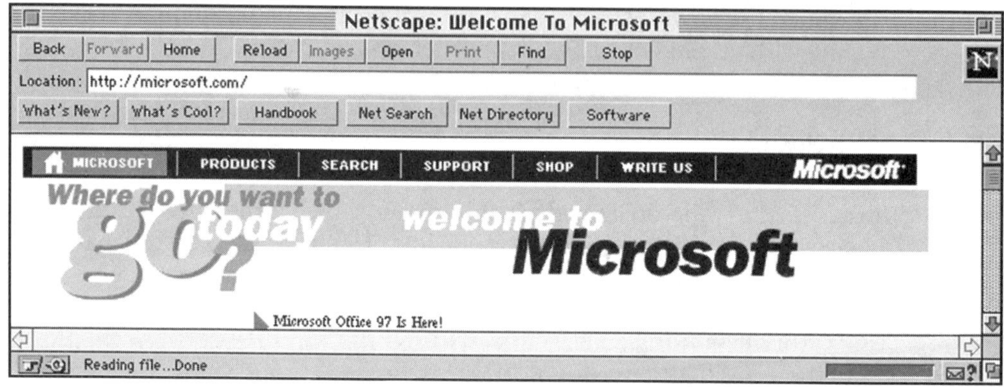

Check this out: No access to a computer? You can now surf the World Wide Web right from your television with *WebTV* from Philips Magnavox. This ingenious little device plugs into the back of your television set and offers foolproof access to the World Wide Web and e-mail **(http://www.magnavox.com/hottechnology/webtv/webtv.html)**.

If you only have access to a basic shell account, give **Lynx** a try `(http://kufacts.cc.ukans.edu/lynx_help/lynx_help_main.html)`. It's a text-only Web browser, but it's fast and fairly easy to use. And, if you are using Windows, you can supplement it with **SlipKnot** `(http://plaza.interport.net/slipknot/slipknot.html)`, which magically allows you to view graphics while using Lynx.

Tip: If you have access only to a text-only terminal connection, don't despair; TIA has arrived! *The Internet Adapter* is a program that emulates a SLIP/PPP connection, providing access to all the fun and exciting Internet software **(http://marketplace.com/)**.

The Web Address

Accessing another Web site is as easy as a click of your mouse. However, there may be times when you will need to manually enter a **URL**, or Uniform Resource Locator (pronounced U-R-L). Here, for example, is the URL, or Web address, to my home page, The ESL Cafe:

`http://www.eslcafe.com`

`http` stands for Hypertext Transfer Protocol and is necessary for connecting to Web pages across the globe.

`://` comes next and is an essential part of the address.

Finally comes the site where the Web page is actually located, as in **`www.eslcafe.com`**

Tip: If you're not able to connect to a site and you believe that the address might be wrong, don't give up. Try connecting to the site again. Once connected, enter the remaining directory names one by one until you find a link to the correct URL.

Some Cool Tips

- It's easy to lose track of where you've been while surfing the Web, so make sure that you create **bookmarks** (or "**favorites**" with Microsoft Explorer). This will enable you to effortlessly return to your favorite sites on future visits.
- When you get tired of waiting for a page to load, try pressing the **Stop** button.
- Take advantage of the **Back** and **Forward** buttons for easier navigation.
- With Netscape and Explorer, you don't need the **`http://`** when manually entering a URL. For example, just typing **`www.eslcafe.com`** gets you to my home page.
- You can have more than one browser open at the same time. For Netscape, choose **New Browser** from the **File** menu. On Explorer, choose **New Window** from the **File** menu.
- Looking for some particular text on a Web page? Go to the **Edit** menu and choose **Find**. If it's there, you'll find it.

Terms You Should Know

- **cache** Pronounced "cash." This is the area of your computer's hard drive that temporarily stores a Web page's text and graphics so that it loads quickly on your next visit.
- **frames** A section of a Web page, with each frame containing its own distinct URL, allowing users to scroll through multiple sites simultaneously.
- **Java** A programming language from Sun Microsystems that allows users to run a variety of programs on the World Wide Web. Java is, to say the least, very hot at the moment.
- **tables** Tables visibly organize information by separating data into rows and columns.

Beyond the Web

One of the many benefits of using the the Web is that you can easily access most of the major Internet applications right from your Web browser, including:

`mailto://`

This enables you to send e-mail.

`news://`

This enables you to read USENET news.

`telnet://`

This enables you to log in to another computer on the Internet.

`gopher://`

This enables you to access gopher-space.

`ftp://`

This enables you to download files from the Internet by the File Transfer Protocol (**FTP**).

Helper Applications and Plug-ins

Helper applications are applications that can be called upon by your Web browser when needed, such as when you want to play a particular sound, graphic, or video file.

The process of setting up helpers is different from browser to browser, but you usually have to do something like this: open **General Preferences** in the **Options** menu, and choose **Helpers**. You'll see a selection of data types in the form. Choose the correct application located on your hard disk that can read the data type, and you're all set!

Tip: A list of Helper applications for Windows, Macintosh, and UNIX (as well as help on configuration) can be found at Netscape's *Help Applications* **(http://home.netscape.com/assist/helper_apps/index.html)**.

Plug-ins, like helper applications, are programs that extend the usefulness of your Web browser in a certain way, such as allowing you to hear live audio broadcasts or view video movies. But unlike helpers, plug-in applications are often displayed right on the Web page. Currently, there are over 96 plug-ins, all of which can be downloaded from Netscape **(http://home.netscape.com/comprod/mirror/navcomponents_download.html)**.

Some of the best include:

Adobe's Acrobat Amber
(http://www.adobe.com/Amber/)
A PDF (portable document format) reader that enables you to view elaborate electronic documents stored in the PDF format.

Macromedia's Shockwave
(http://www.macromedia.com/Tools/Shockwave/sdc/Plugin/)
Offers live animation, multimedia, and sound. Truly amazing!

RealAudio from Progressive Networks
(http://www.realaudio.com/products/ra2.0/)
Lets you experience live audio over the Web.

Stream Works from Xing Software
(www.xingtech.com)
Plays live-on-demand audio and video streams from around the world.

CoolTalk
(http://home.netscape.com/comprod/products/navigator/version_3.0/linefeedcommunication/cooltalk/)
Bundled with Netscape Navigator 3.0, CoolTalk provides Audio Conferencing which enables you to talk to users from around the world; an Answering Machine, which records messages and caller information while you're away; a Shared Whiteboard, where two people across the world can view the same graphic image and even edit it in real time with a variety of tools; and a Chat Tool, which lets you send and receive typed messages, as well as entire text files. Very cool indeed!

Kids Will Be Kids: A Lesson in Cybersafety

Recently, while teaching an Internet seminar to a group of English language students, I left the room for a few minutes and, upon my return, found the entire class hovered around a computer. "What are they doing?" I wondered. Well, they were looking at pictures of Brad Pitt in the nude! Educational? You decide that. There is software, however, that can prevent this kind of experience; it's called **Surf Watch** (www.surfwatch.com). Surf Watch filters and blocks access to objectionable material on the Internet, which is especially useful for those teaching K–12. It's easy to install and available for both the PC and the Macintosh.

Tip: Spend some time at the excellent *Child Safety on the Information Highway* **(http://www.4j.lane.edu/InternetResources/Safety/Safety.html)**, which discusses the benefits of the Internet for kids, as well as the risks and how to prevent them.

Further Help

You can never get enough help, right? Here are some exceptional Web sites that will make your Internet experience a lot more enjoyable.

Beginners Central
(http://www.digital-cafe.com/~webmaster/begin00.html)
This is a dynamite site that gently walks you through your beginning steps on the Internet.

Online Support Center
(http://www.onlinesupport.com/)
Free online support for your Internet questions via e-mail or a Web-messaging area.

WWW FAQ
(http://www.boutell.com/faq/)
This colossal list of frequently asked questions and answers is maintained by Thomas Boutell. If you can't find an answer here, you're not going to find it anywhere!

Finding Resources and Information

"*The internet is such an amazing, seemingly infinite collection of resources. With access to all this information, I and our teachers can be more creative, up-to-date, and 'cool.'*"

Kim Gray
Associate Director, IELS Language School
Austin, Texas

It's easy to find the Internet overwhelming, with its vast and seemingly infinite amount of information and resources. Luckily, there are tools—**Search Engines, Directories, Libraries,** and **White Pages**—that can help you find what you're looking for, whether it's your colleague's e-mail address, particular ESL software, or information on teaching abroad.

Search Engines

With millions of Web pages in Cyberspace, how are you ever going to find what you're looking for? Don't despair, search engines have come to your rescue. Sometimes called "spiders" or "crawlers," search engines continuously visit Web sites on the Internet and create searchable catalogs of Web pages. With a little practice, you'll find search engines to be your most valuable tool on the Internet.

Search engines are very easy to use: you enter their Web page, type your query into a box, click on the submit button, and in seconds a list of matching clickable links appears.

Tip: To make your search a little easier, consider the following:

- What keywords should you use?
- What synonyms would help?
- What different word forms are there?
- Will a phrase help the search?
- Where should I search?

And don't forget to check out VOLTERRE-FR's excellent *Searching Tips* **(http://www.wfi.fr/volterre/searchtips.html)**.

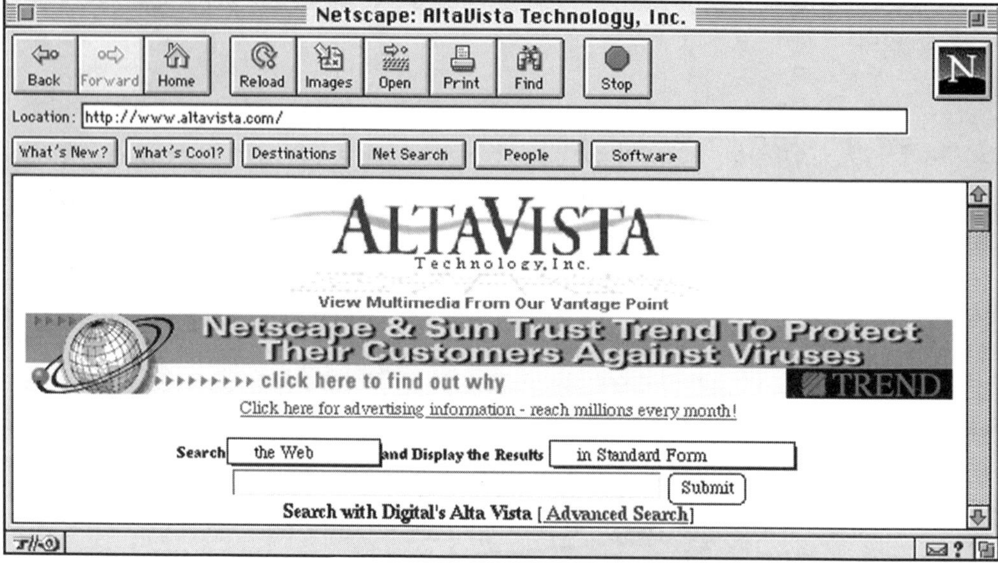

Some of the most popular search engines include:

AltaVista
`(http://www.altavista.digital.com)`
My personal favorite, this lightning-fast search engine has over 8 billion words covering over 30 million Web pages, as well as a full-text index of more than 13,000 newsgroups.

Tip: Roy Bowers has some excellent tips on searching with AltaVista **(http://www.tnis.net/rbowers/search.html)**.

Deja News
`(http://www.dejanews.com/)`
A great resource for searching and reading USENET newsgroups.

Education World Search Engine
`(http://www.education-world.com)`
Search a database of more than 20,000 educational Web sites.

Excite
`(http://www.excite.com)`
Excite has full text to over 11.5 million pages and is updated weekly. You'll also find newsgroups, classifieds, site reviews, news, and columns.

HotBot
(http://www.hotbot.com/)
Stop the press! With over 54 million documents, I think I may have stumbled upon the most complete listing of Web sites in the world! Highly recommended!

Infoseek
(http://www2.infoseek.com/)
Voted the top search engine by *PC Computing*, it also has a a guide to the "best of the Web."

Infoseek Ultra
(http://ultra.infoseek.com/)
A fast and furious new search engine from Infoseek.

Lycos
(http://lycos.cs.cmu.edu/)
Lycos is one of the biggest.

Open Text
(http://www.opentext.com/)
Open Text searches the text of over 21 billion words in its expanding database.

Veronica Gateway
(http://neumann.math.klte.hu/veronica.html)
You can easily search gopherspace from this very easy-to-use search page.

WebCrawler
(http://webcrawler.com/)
This search engine is owned by America Online and includes a list of the 25 most visited sites on the Web.

Tip: For more help on all of the major search engines, visit Terry Gray's *How to Search the Web: A Guide To Search Tools* **(http://issfw.palomar.edu/Library/TGSEARCH.HTM)**.

Multiple Simultaneous Search Engines

These amazing search engines enable you to search several of the major search engines simultaneously. The search takes more time, but the results can be dazzling!

MetaCrawler
(http://metacrawler.cs.washington.edu:8080/)
This speedy engine even allows you to limit the search to your own country, continent, or domain.

Savvy Search
(http://www.cs.colostate.edu/~dreiling/smartform.html)
One of the first simultaneous search tools, Savvy Search conducts searches in 18 different languages.

USE It!
(http://www.he.net/~kamus/useen.htm)
Very well designed, this search engine also can also search in French and Italian.

Tip: Don't forget to visit my very own *ESL Search Page* **(http://www.pacificnet.net/~sperling/search.html)**, where you can easily search MetaCrawler, Savvy Search, Yahoo, InfoSeek, Open Text, Lycos, WebCrawler, AltaVista, Galaxy, and Deja News.

Directories

Directories, unlike search engines, are created by humans (rather than robots) that organize Web pages into various categories, sometimes with reviews and ratings of Web sites. Some of the best include:

A2Z
`(http://a2z.lycos.com/)`
This directory is from the popular Lycos search engine.

Excite NetDirectory
`(http://www.excite.com/)`
Includes site reviews, a guide to over 3,000 destinations, news, and a reference section.

GNN Select
`(http://www.webcrawler.com/)`
At GNN Select you'll find a review of the Web's best sites and programs.

InfoSeek Select Sites
`(http://guide.infoseek.com/)`
Categories include Arts & Entertainment; Business & Finance; Computers & Internet; Education; Government & Politics; Health & Medicine; Living; News; Reference; Science & Technology; Sports; and Travel.

Magellan
`(http://www.mckinley.com/)`
One of the most popular guides on the Web, Magellan includes categories such as Arts, Business, Communications, Computing, Daily Living, Economics, Education, Employment, Entertainment, Environment, Food, Health, Humanities, Internet, KidZone, Law, Mathematics, Music, News, Politics, Pop Culture, Science, Spirituality, Sports, Technology, and Travel.

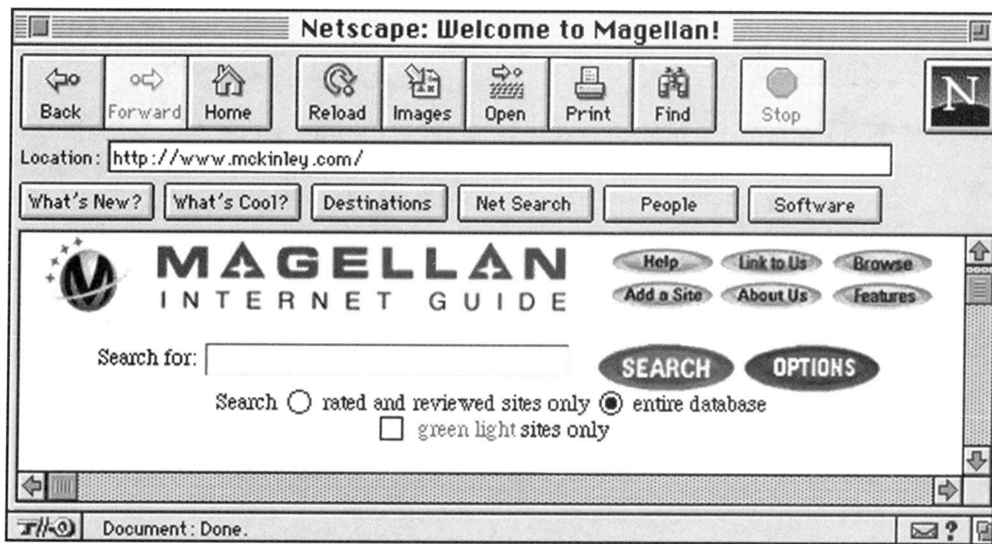

Point
(http://www.pointcom.com/)
Explore an extensive list of sites that the editors of *Point* placed in the top 5 percent.

Yahoo
(http://www.yahoo.com/)
Yahoo has been around since 1994 and is one of the oldest and best-loved Web directories. A stunning collection of Web sites are organized into hundreds of categories and updated daily. There is also a special directory for kids, called Yahooligans. Don't miss it!

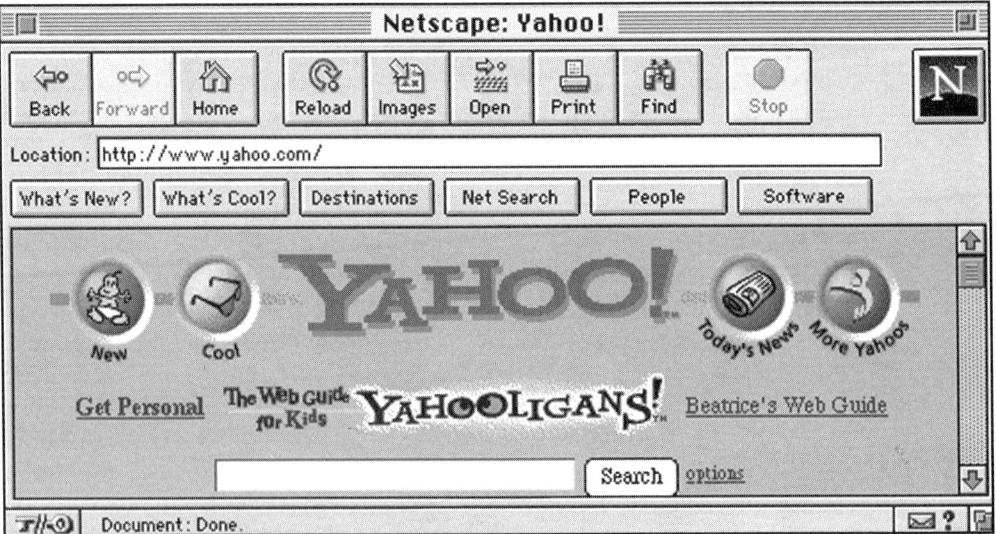

Libraries

"*Look at it this way: When people connect to the Internet, they instantly have access to the information on millions of computers worldwide. With a few touches at a keyboard, a person can get access to material in Australia, the United States, Europe, Asia, Africa, almost anywhere.*"

Elizabeth Reid
"*Writing on the Net*"

The Internet is a terrific resource for accessing full-text newspapers, magazines, journals, reference works, and even books. But where do you begin? An online library is a good place to start your journey.

Some of the finest include:

Electric Library
(http://www.elibrary.com/)
This astonishing resource searches the full text of 150 newspapers and newswires, nearly 800 magazines and journals, 3,000 reference works, and works of literature and art. The first week is free, but after that it's $9.95 per month.

Internet Public Library
(http://ipl.sils.umich.edu/)
This virtual library is the the first public library "of and for the Internet community." Areas include a Reference Center, Youth Services, Teen Services, Classroom, Exhibit Hall, Reading Room, and their own MOO (Multiuser Object-Oriented) environment.

Search ERIC
(http://ericae2.educ.cua.edu/search.htm)
Look through ERIC's bibliographic database of over 850,000 conference papers, reports, instructional materials, research articles, and other materials.

WWW Virtual Library
(http://www.w3.org/pub/DataSources/bySubject/Overview.html)
Started by CERN in 1993, this subject catalog has thousands of links.

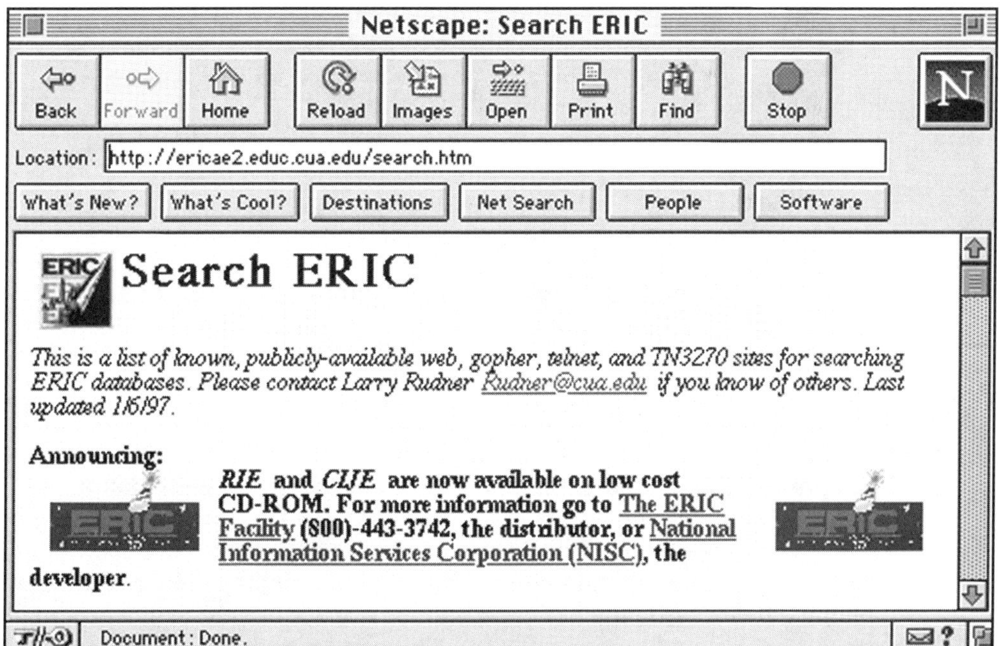

White Pages: Finding People

There will be times when you need to track down a friend's e-mail address, home page, or perhaps even a telephone number. Sure you can pick up the telephone, but White Pages are more powerful and fun! Some of my favorites include:

Bigfoot
(http://www.bigfoot.com/)
E-mail directory that claims to be the "easiest, fastest, friendliest and most comprehensive people directory service on the Net."

Switchboard
(http://www.switchboard.com/)
Look up names and addresses of over 90 million names and 10 million businesses across the U.S.A. for free. One of the best.

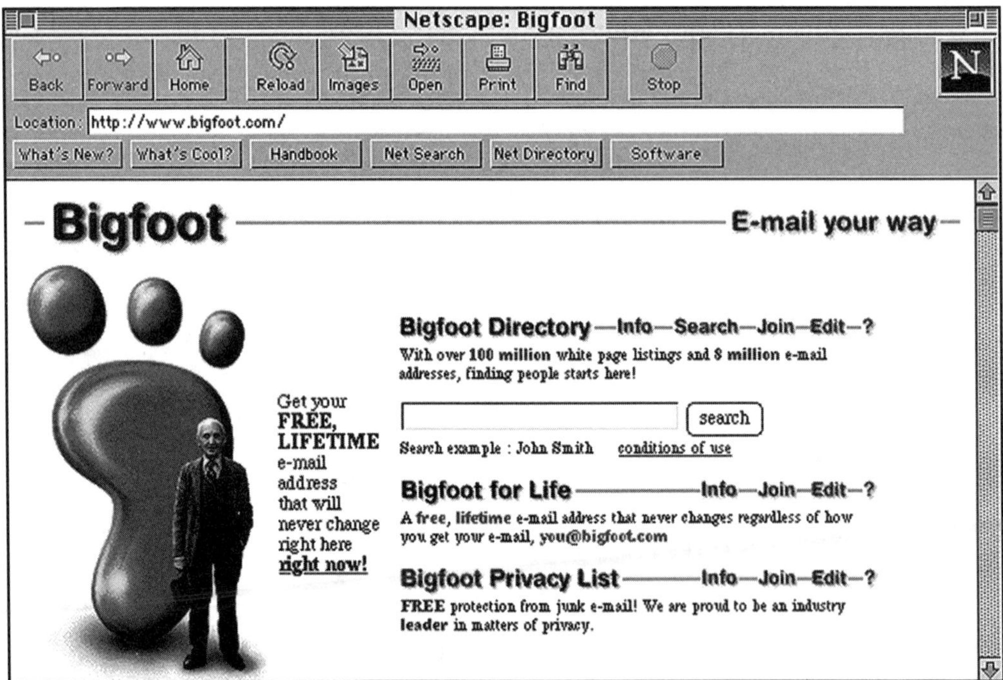

Telephone Directories on the Net
(http://www.procd.com/hl/direct.htm)
Very comprehensive listing of telephone directories on the Net.

Usenet Addresses Services
(http://usenet-addresses.mit.edu/)
Search for e-mail addresses when you know the name of a person or the name of the organization that provides their net access.

WhoWhere
(http://www.whowhere.com/)
In English, Spanish, or French, you can search for e-mail addresses, homepages, companies, and telephone numbers. Very powerful and accurate.

Finding Software

"*We were looking for a classroom management software and posted a query. An hour after posting there was the first answer from New Zealand.*"

Lily Vered
The Open University of Israel, English Department
lilyve@oumail.openu.ac.il

Whether you're using Windows or a Mac, you'll find a mind-boggling assortment of quality software available on the Net, some of it free (**freeware**), some for a price (**shareware**), and some of it for testing (**demos**). Here are some of the top sources for searching Cyberspace for software:

Filez.com
(http://www.filez.com/)
Located in Norway, Filez.com searches over 60 million files and 4000 FTP servers. Truly one of the hottest software search engines around.

Nerd's Heaven Software Directory
(http://boole.stanford.edu/nerdsheaven.html)
This has got to be the most comprehensive collection of software links anywhere in the world. Highly recommended!

Shareware.com
(http://search.shareware.com/SW/FD/Home/)
You can search, browse, and download shareware from all over the world.

Snoopie
(http://www.snoopie.com/)
Claims to be the Internet's most comprehensive file search, and I don't doubt it!

Tip: Download means to transfer a file from the Internet onto your own computer, and the easiest way to accomplish this is right from your Web browser. Just click on the link to the software you want and wait for the download. You may need another utility to decompress the file. Macintosh users should try *Stuffit Expander* (**http://www.aladdinsys.com/consumer/expander1.html**), and Windows users should try *WinZip* (**http://www.winzip.com/**).

Watch out: When downloading over the Internet, you need to be on the lookout for computer *viruses*, which are programs designed to cause damage to your computer and its software. Virus scanning software can usually save the day, so surf over to *Antivirus Resources* **(http://www.hitchhikers.net/av.shtml)** for the latest information and software.

Language Learning Software

"*I've downloaded all sorts of information and lesson plans from all sorts of sites on the Internet. I'm not terribly Web-oriented, as I don't have a graphical interface, but that hasn't really stopped me.*"

Meg Gam
American Language Institute, New York
teacher@amanda.dorsai.org

There's a lot of excellent ESL/EFL and Computer Assisted Language Learning (CALL) software spread out all over the Internet, but finding exactly what you want isn't always easy. Here are some places that will make your journey a lot easier.

CELIA
(http://www.latrobe.edu.au/www/education/celia/celia.html)
CELIA is an archive of software for English as a Second Language, maintained by the Graduate School of Education, La Trobe University, Melbourne, Australia. A must for anyone interested in English language software.

ESL Shareware Tokyo
(http://www2.gol.com/users/tdunnam/eslshareware.html)
Great selection of Mac ESL/EFL software.

Macintosh Software for English Language Learners/Teachers
(http://dspace.dial.pipex.com/town/parade/aag10/)
If you have a Mac, this is another really good place to explore. Splendid collection from Geoff Taylor.

Virtual CALL Library
(http://www.sussex.ac.uk/langc/CALL.html)
Probably the best collection of Computer Aided Language Learning (CALL) software in the world. Don't miss it!

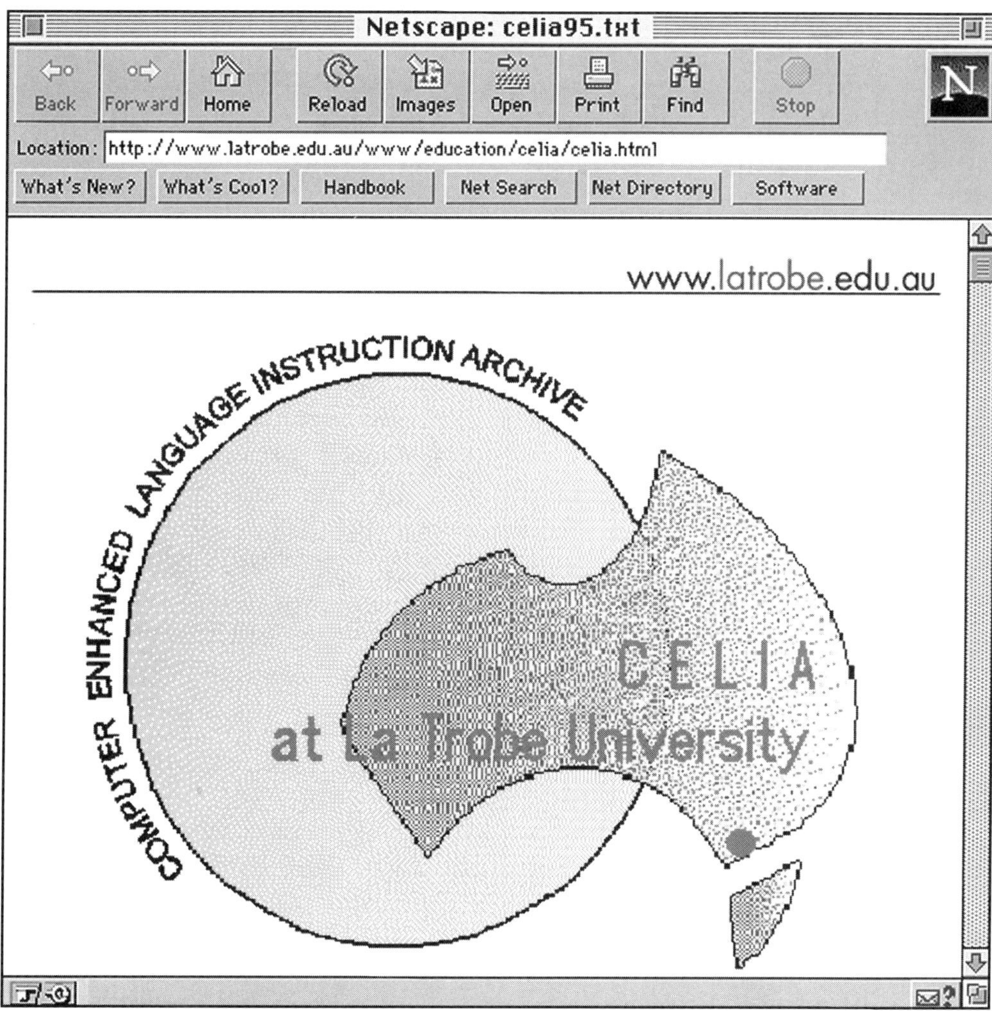
Netscape: celia95.txt
Back
Forward
Home
Reload
Images
Open
Print
Find
Stop
Location: http://www.latrobe.edu.au/www/education/celia/celia.html
What's New?
What's Cool?
Handbook
Net Search
Net Directory
Software
www.latrobe.edu.au
COMPUTER ENHANCED LANGUAGE INSTRUCTION ARCHIVE
CELIA
at La Trobe University

Yamada Language Center Font Archive
(`http://babel.uoregon.edu/Yamada/fonts.html`)
This is the place to go if you are looking for non-English fonts. Wonderful resource!

More Places to Search

Area Code Decoder
(`http://www.xmission.com/~americom/aclookup.html`)
Quickly decoded U.S. area codes.

AT&T's Toll-free Directory
(`http://www.tollfree.att.net/dir800/`)
Easily search for toll-free telephone numbers.

BigBook Map Server
(`http://www.bigyellow.com/`)
Displays a map for any U.S. address.

CD Search
(`http://blueridge.infomkt.ibm.com/knudsen/cdsearch.html`)
Searches more than 100,000 CD music titles.

Domain Name Search
(`http://www.internet.org/cgi-bin/genobject/domains`)
The complete database contains data for over 410,000 domain names.

Electronic Journals
(`http://www.edoc.com/ejournal/`)
Search a huge database of online journals.

Games Domain Search
(http://www.gamesdomain.co.uk/)
Search a database of games and games-related information.

Globewide Network Academy Course Catalog
(http://catalog.gnacademy.org/cgi-bin/cgiwrap/gnacademy/catsearch)
Search for online and distance learning courses.

Government Publications
(http://lib-www.ucr.edu/govinfo.html)
Search for government publications available on the Net.

HYTELNET
(http://galaxy.einet.net/hytelnet/START.TXT.html)
Search all Internet-accessible libraries, Free-nets, Bulletin Board Systems (BBSs), and other information sites by Telnet.

Internet Movie Database
(http://us.imdb.com/)
Search the world's largest database of movie information.

Internet Sleuth
(http://www.isleuth.com/)
This "database of databases" searches over 1,500 searchable databases.

The List
(http://thelist.iworld.com/)
Search a list of over 3,799 Internet Service Providers.

Lists of Lists
(http://catalog.com/vivian/interest-group-search.html)
Search thousands of Internet mailing lists.

Princeton Review College Search
(http://www.review.com/)
Search reviews and links to colleges and universities.

Publishing Companies Online
(http://www.edoc.com/ejournal/publishers.html)
Search all publishers that are online.

WebWeather
(http://www.webwx.com/)
Check the latest U.S. weather forecast.

Worldwide Events Database
(http://www.ipworld.com/EVENTS/SEARCH.HTM)
Search events happening around the world.

ZD Net
(http://home.zdnet.com/home/filters/main.html)
Search all of the several publications from Ziff-Davis.

Communicating on the Net

“*The Internet has put me in touch with colleagues all over the world and given me access to their ideas and a tap into their creativity.*”

Renee Wahl
Amit Technological High School at Bar Ilan University
Ranat Gan, Israel
wahl@inter.net.il

Sure, there's an abundance of information waiting for you on the Internet, but even more powerful and exciting is the opportunity for you and your class to meet, communicate, and interact with millions of others from around the world. This chapter will show you how by looking at:

- **E-mail** — You can instantly send and receive electronic mail from around the world.
- **Mailing lists** — Through e-mail, you can participate in discussions on thousands of topics.
- **USENET news** — You can read and post messages on almost every imaginable topic.
- **Web discussion boards** — From your Web browser, you can read and post messages on a variety of topics.
- **Chat** — You can participate in live conversations, using text, audio, and even video.
- **MOOs** — MUD Object Oriented, where several people can interact with one another simultaneously.

E-mail

E-mail, or Electronic Mail, is the most popular way to communicate on the Internet and is usually the first Internet application new users learn. Once you get used to instantly sending and receiving messages across the world, post office mail (or “snail mail,” as it's called on the Net) will seem like something from the distant past.

Tip: No access to e-mail? At *HotMail* (**http://www.hotmail.com**) you can get a free Web-based e-mail account accessible worldwide from any computer.

To send a message, you first need to know someone's e-mail address, which has three parts:

Username @ Machine Address

Username is a unique name assigned by an Internet provider.
My username is *sperling*.

@ is the "at" symbol and is needed on every e-mail address after the username (kind of like a postage stamp).

The Machine Address is the address to which you want to send the e-mail message.
My address is `eslcafe.com`

So, my e-mail address looks like this:
`sperling@eslcafe.com`

Tip: Practice by sending me an e-mail message at **`sperling@eslcafe.com`**, and I promise to write you back!

Watch out: Be careful when typing a person's e-mail address. One typo will cause the message to come bouncing back to you, never reaching its destination. For example, spaces aren't allowed in an e-mail address.

Though your e-mail software may be slightly different, here are some of the common operations:

To: Here you enter the person's e-mail address.
From: Your e-mail address (usually automatically filled in).
Subject: You can put anything here. Be creative!
Cc: Carbon Copy, meaning that you can send the same letter to several different people.
Bcc: This is Blind Carbon Copy. As with a Carbon Copy, you can send the same letter to several different people, but with a Blind Carbon Copy, the recipients of your message will not know if the message was sent to only them or to several people.
Attachments: You can attach documents, files, graphics, sound, and even software.

In addition, most e-mail programs allow you to:

- **Send mail** — The letter is sent to its destination in Cyberspace.
- **Receive mail** — You can receive mail addressed to your e-mail account.
- **Reply** — You can respond to e-mail you've received.
- **Forward** — You can send a received e-mail message to another person.

- **Save** — you can save e-mail you've received.
- **Print** — you can print e-mail you've received.
- **Address Book** — you can store e-mail addresses.

Here's an example of an e-mail message from me to my wife:

```
        To: dao@aol.com
      From: sperling@eslcafe.com
   Subject: Late Again!
        Cc:
       Bcc:
Attachment:
      Body: Hi Dao,
            Looks like I'll be home a little late because
            I've got to help a student with his e-mail.
            See you soon,
            Dave
            ************************************************
            California State University, Northridge
            Dave's ESL Cafe on the Web:
            http://www.eslcafe.com/
            ************************************************
```

Tip: Notice the signature at the end of the message? They're very common in Cyberspace. Want to create one of your own? With Eudora, from the menu, choose Windows, then Signature. Create your signature and save it. With Pine, go to your UNIX prompt and type: **`pico.signature`** Create your signature, press Ctrl+x, and save it. Easy, isn't it?

Watch out: E-mail messages are somewhat like postcards: you never know who might read the message. Be careful what you write, or you may find yourself in trouble.

Using E-mail in the Classroom

"One of the things I use the Internet for is to keep my new arrivals in contact with their homeland because middle school kids have a hard time making that transition— more so than many other age groups, because these kids are seeking an identity, trying to find out who they are."

Lynore Carnuccio
Mustang Public Schools, Mustang, Oklahoma
nuch@flash.net

With the ability to instantly and easily communicate with classes from almost anywhere in the world, your students can exchange messages, as well as participate in discussions with **key pals** (translation: pen pals via the Internet). Here's a list of some of the best locations for you and your class to get started.

A Beginner's Guide to Effective Email
(http://enterprise.powerup.com.au/htmlxp/pu/emailhow.htm)
E-mail is not the same as traditional letter writing, and this is a good place to learn some of the differences.

"*I got e-mail from my father. He typed e-mail to me in English. But his English is difficult for me to understand. I write e-mail the way I speak. My father's English is like the English that I see in a difficult book. So I guess that he looked into the dictionary many times.*"

Tomoki, ESL Student
California State University, Northridge

California Email Project Homepage
(http://www.otan.dni.us/webfarm/emailproject/email.html)
Sponsored by the Outreach Technical Assistance Center and the Staff Development Institute of California, this site gives adult learners a place to showcase their best work.

eMail Classroom Exchange
(http://www.iglou.com/xchange/ece/index.html)
With over 300 schools participating, this is an excellent free resource where classrooms can meet other classrooms from around the world.

E-Mail Key Pal Connection
(http://www.comenius.com/keypal/index.html)
From The Comenius group, $14.95 buys you up to three key pals.

ESL Student Email Connection for Students
(http://www.pacificnet.net/~sperling/student.html)

For Teachers
(http://www.pacificnet.net/~sperling/guestbook.html)
English language students and teachers can automatically add their name and e-mail address to a continuously expanding database of thousands of names from around the world.

HUT Internet Writing Project
(http://www.hut.fi/~rvilmi/Project/)
This project, from Internet pioneer Ruth Vilmi, is "an ongoing international writing project which brings students of universities in Asia, Europe, and North America together via the Internet so that they can share their insights and assist one another in writing in English on a wide selection of topics."

Intercultural E-Mail Classroom Connections
(http://www.stolaf.edu/network/iecc/index.html)
A series of four electronic mailing lists that teachers can use for finding classrooms for shared e-mail exchanges.

International E-Mail Tandem Network
(http://www.slf.ruhr-uni-bochum.de/email/infen.html)
A place where universities throughout the world work together using e-mail to assist their students in learning languages in tandem.

Tip: Try communicating with your class by e-mail, either individually or as a group. E-mail is often less threatening, and it's a great way to get shy students to open up.

Mailing Lists

Once you and your students get used to e-mail, you'll quickly want to begin subscribing to **mailing lists**, which are topic-specific discussion groups on almost every imaginable topic.

Watch out: It's easy to subscribe to a lot of interesting mailing lists, but you may soon discover that you are receiving over 200 e-mail messages a day! Don't forget to save the instructions on how to unsubscribe yourself from a list. You can also use *NMCS*, which has a free Web service that automates subscribing and unsubscribing to lists. Just fill out the form **(http://nmcs.clever.net/html/nmcsad/majordomo.shtml)**.

The three most common types of mailing lists are:

- **listserv**
  listserv@address
- **listproc**
  listproc@address
- **majordomo**
  majordomo@address

Mailing lists have two different addresses: The **List Address**, to which you send a message to everyone subscribed to the list; and the **List Server Address**, where you send commands, such as those that subscribe and unsubscribe you from the list. To avoid embarrassment, ***Be careful!***

Finding a List

There are literally thousands of lists waiting for you (and more each day!), so finding the right list isn't always easy. The following services, however, will make your search a lot easier.

Liszt
(http://www.liszt.com/)
Enter any word or phrase to search the world's largest directory of mailing lists— 54,760 listserv, listproc, majordomo and independently managed lists from 1,812 sites.

Publicly Accessible Mailing Lists
(http://www.neosoft.com/internet/paml/bysubj.html)
Browse through thousands of lists sorted by name or subject.

Reference.com
(http://www.reference.com/)
Perform detailed searches on thousands of lists. Highly recommended!

Tile.net Lists
(http://tile.net/lists/)
A reference to all the listserv discussion groups on the Internet.

Student Lists

Students can use mailing lists to keep up with current news, learn new vocabulary, and communicate with students and teachers. Here are some of the best.

Watch out: All commands are put in the body of the e-mail message and the subject of the message needs to be blank, unless otherwise specified. More help can be found at *How to Subscribe to Mailing Lists* (**http://www.dundee.ac.uk/~fmsteink/howto.htm**).

Daily Brief
(http://www.tiac.net/users/incinc/inc/inc_db.html)
Daily summary of U.S. and world news sent out by e-mail every weekday morning.
To subscribe, send the command `subscribe db` (in the Subject of your mail) to: `incinc@tiac.net`

EslList
A moderated list for 11- to 16-year-old English language learners open to topics of interest to children around the world.
To subscribe to EslList, send an e-mail message to: `macjord@oxnardsd.org`
Example:
`subscribe EslList Dave Sperling`

esol
Discussion for ESOL/Bilingual Graduate students.
Mail the command `info esol` to `majordomo@lists.umbc.edu`

explore-l
ESL student discussion list.
Mail the command `information explore-l` to `listproc@hawaii.edu`

SL-LISTS
(http://www.latrobe.edu.au/www/education/sl/sl.html)
Excellent series of discussion lists for English language students brought to you by Latrobe University in Australia.
Mail the the command `info ENGL-SL` to: `listserv@lugb.latrobe.edu.au`
The lists include:

INTRO-SL Discussion list for new members

CHAT-SL General discussion list (low level)

DISCUSS-SL General discussion list (high level)

BUSINESS-SL Discussion list on business and economics

ENGL-SL Discussion list on learning English

EVENT-SL Discussion list on current events

MOVIE-SL Discussion list on the cinema

MUSIC-SL Discussion list on music

SCITECH-SL Discussion list on science, technology, & computers

SPORT-SL Discussion list on sports

Word.A.Day
Mails out an English vocabulary word and its definition each day.
To subscribe, send e-mail to `wsmith@wordsmith.org`, and on the Subject line, put `subscribe (your full name here)`.

Teacher Lists

Hey, there's plenty of great lists for you, too! Here is a selection of some of the best ESL/EFL-oriented lists for teachers.

aaiep-l
American Association of Intensive English Programs members list.
Mail the command `information aaiep-l` to `listproc2@bgu.edu`

ACW-L
The Alliance for Computers and Writing e-mail discussion list.
`(http://english.ttu.edu/acw/)`
Subscribe to the list by sending an e-mail message to: `listproc@listserv.ttu.edu` with the following message: `subscribe acw-l yourfirstname yourlastname`

aep
Academic English discussion list.
Mail the command `information aep` to `listproc@u.washington.edu`

alesl
Applied linguistics/ESL list.
Mail the command *information alesl* to `listproc@sphinx.gsu.edu`

ATEG
Assembly for the Teaching of English Grammar.
Mail the command *info ATEG* to `listserv@miamiu.acs.muohio.edu`

Bilingual
`(http://www.sover.net/~globalad/bilingual.html)`
Forum on bilingual education and language planning at the Hong Kong Institute of Education.
To subscribe, send an e-mail message to `majordomo@ied.edu.hk` and leave the subject line blank. At the body of the message, type `subscribe bilingual`

CETEFL-L
List for Central European teachers.
Mail the command *info CETEFL-L* to
listserv@cesnet.cz

CTESL-L
An international online fellowship for Christians who teach English language.
Mail the command *info ctesl-l* to
majordomo@iclnet93.iclnet.org

EFELLOWS
Peer Collaboration method of English Language Instruction.
Mail the command *info EFELLOWS* to
listserv@uriacc.uri.edu

ELTASIA-L
A discussion list about English language teaching in Asia.
Mail the command *info eltasia-l* to
majordomo@nucleus.nectec.or.th

ENGLED-L
English education.
Mail the command *info ENGLED-L* to
listserv@psuvm.psu.edu

english
English language teaching list.
Mail the command *information english* to listproc@bilkent.edu.tr

ESLCC
English as a Second Language at the Community Colleges.
Mail the command *info FLTEACH* to
eslcc-request@hcc.hawaii.edu

esl-sne
English as a second language.
Mail the command *information esl-sne* to listproc@schoolnet.ca

esltech
ESL Teachers' Technology Group.
Mail the command *info esltech* to
majordomo@darkwing.uoregon.edu

EST-L
Teachers of English for Science and Technology.
Mail the command *info EST-L* to
listserv@asuvm.inre.asu.edu

FLteach
(http://www.cortland.edu/www_root/flteach/flteach.html)
Foreign language teachers' forum.
Mail the command *info FLTEACH* to
listserv@ubvm.cc.buffalo.edu

GLESOL-L
Discussion list for gay, lesbian, bisexual educators of English to speakers of other languages.
To subscribe, leave the subject blank and type as the first line of the message: *subscribe glesol-l* to
mailserv@uni.edu

Global Schoolnet Mailing Lists
(http://www.gsn.org/gsn/archives/index.html)
Excellent series of educational mailing lists.

grammar-l
English grammar for teachers of English language.
Mail the command *information grammar-l* to listproc@sphinx.gsu.edu

hhpub
English language teaching materials.
Mail the command *information hhpub* to listproc@sphinx.gsu.edu

IECC-Projects
Projects in the intercultural e-mail classroom.
`iecc-projects-request@stolaf.edu`

KEXPAT
Discussion on working and living in Korea.
Subscribe by writing to
`kexpat-request@nextel.net`
In the body of your message, write *subscribe kexpat*

LATTICE
Several linguistics-related lists from The Language and Technology Centre of the National Languages and Literacy Institute of Australia, for language, literacy, and linguistics specialists, from the University of Queensland in Brisbane, Australia.
To subscribe to the lists, send an e-mail message with a blank subject line to:
`majordomo@cltr.uq.oz.au`
The body of the message should read:
subscribe [name of list]
The lists include APPLIX, a discussion group for people interested in applied linguistics, and ATELL, a discussion group for people interested in computer-assisted language learning.

LINGUIST
(`http://www.ling.rochester.edu/linguist/contents.html`)
The LINGUIST discussion list.
Mail the command *info LINGUIST* to
`listserv@tamvm1.tamu.edu`

LLTI
(`http://eleazar.dartmouth.edu/IALL/index.html`)
Language Learning Technology International.
To subscribe, send the following message to:
`listserv@dartmouth.edu`
SUB LLTI yourID@hostname yourfirstname yourlastname

LTEST-L
Discussion list of the International Language Testing Association (ILTA).
Mail the command *info LTEST-L* to
`listserv@psuvm.psy.edu`

Multicultural Education List
A discussion of multicultural education.
To subscribe, enter only the following command in the BODY of your e-mail message to
`listserv@ubvm.cc.buffalo.edu`: *Sub Mult-Cul yourfirstname yourlast name*

Multicultural Pavilion
(`http://curry.edschool.virginia.edu:80/go/multicultural/home.html`)
A resource for educators interested in multicultural issues.
To subscribe, send the following message to `majordomo@virginia.edu`:
subscribe mcpavilion your e-mail address

Neteach-L
(`http://thecity.sfsu.edu/~funweb/neteach.htm`)
A list for international teachers of English as a second or foreign language to discuss Internet-assisted teaching and learning. Highly recommended!
Mail the command *information neteach-l* to `listserv@thecity.sfsu.edu`

OCC-L
On-Line College Classroom list.
Mail the command *information occ-l* to
`listproc@hawaii.edu`

prepare-l
English preparation for English language teachers.
Mail the command *information prepare-l* to `listproc@sphinx.gsu.edu`

SCOLT
Southern Conference on Language Teaching.
Mail the command *information scolt* to `listserv@catfish.valdosta.peachnet.edu`

SLART-L
Second Language Acquisition Research and/or Teaching.
Mail the command *info SLART-L* to `listserv@cunyvm.cuny.edu`

TESL-L
Teachers of English as a Second Language list.
Mail the command *info TESL-L* to `listserv@cunyvm.cuny.edu`
TESL-L Branches include:

- TESLCA-L TESL and Technology Branch of TESL-L list.
- TESLFF-L Fluency First and Whole Language Online seminar.
- TESLIE-L Intensive English program.
- TESLIT-L Adult education and literacy.
- TESLJB-L Jobs and employment issues.
- TESLMW-L Materials writers.
- TESP-L English for specific purposes.)

Note: *You must subscribe to TESL-L before you can subscribe to its branches.*

TESLK-12
Teachers of English as a second language to children.
Mail the command *info TESLK-12* to `listserv@cunyvm.cuny.edu`

Words-L
Discussion on words.
Mail the command *info WORDS-L* to `listserv@uga.cc.uga.edu`

WRICOM
Discussion of issues associated with computers in writing, writing instruction, and social and cognitive factors affecting the writing process.
To join, send e-mail to: `mailbase@mailbase.ac.uk`
with the following message in the body of your e-mail: *join wricom your-first-name your-last-name*

WWWEDU (World Wide Web in Education list)
(`http://k12.cnidr.org:90/wwwedu.html`)
Discussion on the potential of World Wide Web use in education.
To join WWWEDU, send a message to `listproc@educom.unc.edu` and in the body of the message write:
subscribe wwwedu (your name)

Tip: From a single page, you can easily subscribe and unsubscribe to many of the above mailing lists at Kristina Harris's *Linguistic Funland* (**`http://math.unr.edu/linguistics/tesllist.html`**).

USENET Newsgroups

"*Internet use and newsgroup participation have helped me improve my teaching by giving me access to a wide range of information: information that in most cases would be unavailable or difficult to access. Newsgroup participation helps you keep up to date with new pedagogical and technological advances.*"

Mark Peterson
Japan Advanced Institute of Science and Technology
`mark@jaist.ac.jp`

With thousands of topics to choose from, USENET, like e-mail discussion lists, enables you and your students to read and post threaded messages to bulletin board-like newsgroups. They are, in essence, an exciting international meeting spot.

Some of USENET's categories include:

- **comp** computer-related topics
- **news** USENET information
- **biz** Business
- **rec** Recreational activities and hobbies
- **sci** Science
- **soc** Cultures and current events
- **talk** Debates and discussions
- **misc** Discussion on topics that don't fit into other categories
- **alt** Alternative expressions of various subjects
- **clari** A subscription service for commercial wire-service stories
- **k12** Educational subjects relating to K–12 (kindergarten through 12th grade)

To read USENET newsgroup articles, you'll need a newsreading program. The most popular Web browsers have newsreaders automatically built into them, but other alternatives include **Newswatcher** for the Mac (`http://charlotte.acns.nwu.edu/jln/progs.html`) and **Free Agent** for Windows (`http://www.forteinc.com/forte/`).

Tip: If you lack access to USENET (but are on the the Web), try using *Deja News* (**`http://www.dejanews.com/`**) and *Reference.com* (**`http://www.reference.com/`**).

Finding a Newsgroup

With over 20,000 newsgroups floating around in Cyberspace, it's not always easy to find what you're looking for. Here are three useful sites to help narrow your search.

Liszt
(http://www.liszt.com/cgi-bin/news.cgi)
Search over 15,000 different newsgroups.

Reference.com
(http://www.reference.com/)
Search and read over 16,000 newsgroups.

Tile.net News
(http://www.tile.net/tile/news/index.html)
Great for searching, but lacks the ability to read the news.

ESL/EFL-related Groups

Here are some USENET newsgroups that will be of interest to ESL/EFL teachers:

alt.education.distance
Distance learning

alt.education.email-project
Collaborative projects shared by e-mail

alt.literacy.adult
Adults, literacy, reading, writing

alt.usage.english
English grammar, word usages, and related topics

bit.listserv.slart-l
Second Language Acquisition Research and Teaching (Moderated)

bit.listserv.tesl-l
Teachers of English as a Second Language (Moderated)

bit.listserv.words-l
English Language discussion group

can.english
About the English-speaking population (in English)

can.schoolnet.english
English elementary/secondary schools curriculum

comp.edu.languages.natural
Computer-assisted languages instruction issues

k12.ed.comp.literacy
Teaching computer literacy in grades K–12

k12.lang.art
The art of teaching language skills in grades K–12

misc.education.language.english
Teaching English to speakers of other languages

misc.writing
Discussion of writing in all of its forms

sci.lang
Natural languages, communication, etc.

Web Discussion Boards

"*I can go on-line at 10 P.M. and see what's going on and share ideas with others all over the world. And I don't have to talk—my voice is overworked as it is.*"

Meg Gam
American Language Institute, New York
teacher@amanda.dorsai.org

Similar to USENET newsgroups, Web boards allow you and your students to easily read and post messages directly onto a Web page from your Web browser. Here are some boards devoted exclusively to English language students and teachers.

ESL Chat Line
(http://www.ritslab.ubc.ca/cgi/esl/esl.html)
A place where students can discuss their understanding of their learning experiences.

ESL Discussion Center
(http://eslcafe.com/discussion)
Student discussion boards include Current Events, Food, Holidays, Learning English, Movies, and Music. Teacher boards include Activities and Games, Computer-Assisted Language Learning, English for Specific Purposes, K–12, Teaching-Learning Material, and Teaching Tips.

ESL Message Exchange
(http://www.pacificnet.net/~sperling/wwwboard/wwwboard.html)
Discuss numerous topics with ESL/EFL students and teachers from around the world. For example,

Posted by Elise on the ESL Message Exchange
(http://www.pacificnet.net/~sperling/wwwboard/wwwboard.html)

"I have some students that are interested in sending letters via e-mail and/or the postal service. The students are mostly 3rd, 4th and 5th graders. They would especially enjoy writing to countries other than the U.S.A., but anyone interested, let me know. My students don't really have a concept of how big the 50 states are either, so let's hear from you!"

ESL Help Center
(http://www.pacificnet.net/~sperling/wwwboard2/wwwboard.html)
Around-the-clock help for ESL students from an international team of ESL/EFL teachers from around the world. For example,

ESL Help Center
(http://www.pacificnet.net/~sperling/wwwboard2/wwwboard.html)

Q: "Is it fine to introduce my female friend to one person using 'my girlfriend'? I've heard it all the time but I'm scared to use it. I live in San Francisco where people get confused about this pretty easily."

DeeVee from Taiwan

A: "Just introduce her as your friend. Friend is gender free. You can also use other phrases like, classmate, colleague, and co-worker which describe more precisely your relationship if you feel it is important to do so."

Sharon Clampitt
Inter American University of Puerto Rico

Live Chat

"*The colleagues I know best, I met online.*"

Miriam Seave
ELI, Wayne State University
mseaver@cms.cc.wayne.edu

Imagine your class having instant *real-time* conversations with other classes across the world, complete with sound, text, images, and even video. Sounds like something from the year 2030? Well, it's all possible now!

Internet Relay Chat (IRC)

Extremely popular (and very addictive), **Internet Relay Chat (IRC)** allows users to select from thousands of channels to talk in real time with users from around the world—kind of like a global Internet conference with people from places as far afield as Canada, Russia, Brazil, and Japan!

Some examples of the many multicultural channels include:

#asian	**#colombia**
#bosnia	**#hmong**
#brasil	**#japan**
#china	**#kuwait**
#chinese	**#laos**

You can also easily create your own channels and have a private chat with friends, teachers, students, and other classes in different places.

Tip: Use IRC to talk with other teachers with Scott Mandel's *Teachers Helping Teachers* (**http://www.pacificnet.net/~mandel/ircinfo.html**).

You can easily "telnet" into an IRC server from most UNIX accounts, but there is software to make the IRC experience a lot easier and more fun. Try:

Global Chat
(http://arachnid.qdeck.com/chat/)
Brought to you by the very innovative Quarterdeck Corporation, this is one of my favorite chat programs because it's free, easy to set up and use, and available for both Windows and Macintosh.

IRCLE
(http://www.ircle.com/)
Excellent Mac software.

mIRC
(http://www.mirc.co.uk/)
Popular for Windows.

Tip: For an academic outlook on IRC, read Elizabeth Reid's two theses and several essays (**http://www.ee.mu.oz.au/papers/emr/index.html**). And for more help and information on IRC, read the excellent *IRC FAQ* (**http://www.kei.com/irc.html**).

Web Chat

You can also experience live chat from your Web browser. It's not quite as fast as IRC, but it's still fun. Best bets include:

OmniChat
(http://www.4-lane.com/)
Chat about business, music, books, writing, computer, politics, and lots more!

ESL Chat Central
(http://www.eslcafe.com/chat)
Live Web-based chat, from Dave's ESL Cafe.

MOOs

"MOOs are hardly ever completely shut down, and they can be programmed and recompiled without losing everything. They grow and grow and, because of their permanent nature, a sense of community and place forms in the minds of the users. This opens up psychological possibilities I see as being difficult if not impossible in IRC. If you log on to a MOO and nobody is there, you still have an incredibly rich environment in which to use language. Just wander around looking at things and running programs that are left lying about!"

Lonnie Turbee
Syracuse University
lmturbee@syr.edu

So what is a MOO? No, it's not a sound that comes out of a cow! A MOO, or MUD Object Oriented, is a virtual environment where people can "talk" to each other in virtual "rooms." It takes a little practice to get the hang of it, and you'll need to **telnet** into a MOO, but the rewards can be truly magical.

Tip: To make your MOO experience a lot easier, try using some MOO software. For a Mac, try *MacMoose* (**http://www.eden.com/~hsoi/mud/**); PC users can try *Winsock Game Clients for Windows* (**http://www.rahul.net/galen/client1.html**).

My favorite MOO in the world is Julie Falsetti's creation called **schMooze University** (**http://schmooze.hunter.cuny.edu:8888/**), a "virtual, friendly, online school for English learning." Yoshi Awaji has created several informative pages about schMooze University, including:

Command Chart
(http://www.cc.rim.or.jp/~awaji/schMOOze/ENG/ocommands.html)
Help on some of the commands necessary to navigate around.

Guest Tour
(http://www.cc.rim.or.jp/~awaji/schMOOze/ENG/tour.html)
A tour of the "campus."

Let's go to schMOOze University!
(http://www.cc.rim.or.jp/~awaji/schMOOze/ENG/general.html)
An introduction to the in's and out's of schMOOze.

Useful Expressions
(http://www.cc.rim.or.jp/~awaji/schMOOze/ENG/tocexp.html)
Lessons of some of schMOOze's lingo.

Another excellent MOO for teachers is called **Netoric**, which is used to discuss issues related to computer-assisted writing instruction. Netoric is very receptive to new visitors, and there are even special events such as the **Netoric's Tuesday Cafe Discussion**. More information can be found on their home page (**http://www.cs.bsu.edu/homepages/siering/netoric.html**).

Finally, there is Jeff Cooper's extensive list of **Educational MOOs** (**`http://math.unr.edu/linguistics/edmoolist.html`**), where you'll find descriptions of over 31 MOOs related to the field of education.

Audio

In case you haven't heard, with some special software, a microphone, and a pair of speakers, you can make Internet-based calls to destinations around the world *without* paying long-distance rates (sounds too good to be true, doesn't it?). And this means that your students can actually experience *voice conversations* with other classes from around the globe!

In recent months, dozens of Net phone products have hit the market. One of the best is **Netphone** (**`http://www.vocaltec.com/`**), which has free demos for both Windows and the Mac.

Other products worth trying include:

Clearphone (Mac)
(`http://www.clearphone.com/`)
A Mac-only phone utility.

CoolTalk
(`http://home.netscape.com/eng/mozilla/3.0/relnotes/windows-3.0b4.html`)
This is definitely a product worth checking out because it comes bundled with Netscape Navigator 3.0 and has versions for UNIX, Windows, and Macintosh.

Digiphone
(`http://www.planeteers.com`)
For Windows and the Mac.

Voice E-Mail
(`http://www.bonzi.com`)
Send your voice, music, and more to friends around the world. PC-only versions available.

WebPhone
(`http://www.itelco.com`)
This slick piece of software was voted Editor's Choice in PC Magazine. PC-only version available.

WebTalk
(`http://arachnid.qdeck.com/qdeck/products/webtalk/`)
Quarterdeck's Internet phone, available only for the PC.

Tip: To keep up with the numerous audio products, visit Voice on Net Home Page (**`http://www.von.com/`**).

Videoconferencing

> *"With technology, and the computer in particular, becoming integral parts of most facets of our lives in the late 20th century, the virtual classroom is on its way to becoming a viable option for the facilitation of learning."*
>
> Karla Frizler, City College of San Francisco
> From *The Internet as an Educational Tool in ESOL Writing Instruction*

The next stage after voice communication is experiencing live ***videoconferencing***. The technology is far from perfect and it may take a bit of trouble to set everything up correctly, but the rewards will be well worth the effort when you and your class visually interact with ESL students and teachers, scientists, politicians, and writers throughout the world.

Aside from a computer and a fast Internet connection (28.8 modem *barely* does it), you'll also need:

- Microphone
- Speakers
- Sound Card (for a PC)
- Camera

Tip: For $99 (black and white) or $199 (color), the Quickcam camera may be just what you need (**http://baby.indstate.edu/msattler/sci-tech/comp/hardware/quickcam.html**).

- Software — One of the most popular programs is **Cu-SeeMe**, created at Cornell University. Try downloading a free demo of this award-winning software at (**http://goliath.wpine.com/cu-seeme.html**).

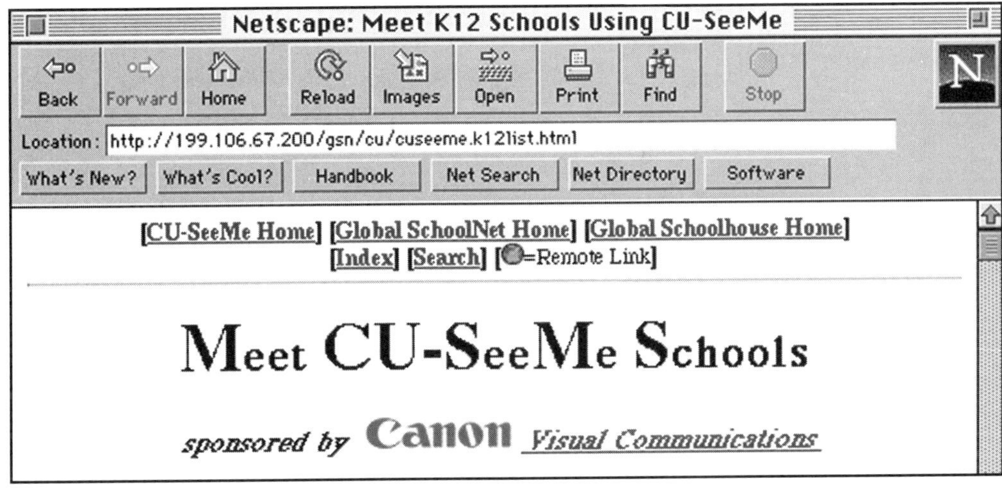

Once you're all set up, you'll need to connect with some classes from different parts of the world. Thank goodness for Meet Schools Using CU-SeeMe (**`http://199.106.67.200/gsn/cu/cuseeme.k12list.html`**), where you'll find a listing of participating classes from Australia, Canada, Denmark, England, Finland, Germany, Ireland, Israel, Japan, Mexico, Norway, Republic of China, Sweden, and the United States.

Netiquette

Finally, I need to touch a little upon Internet etiquette, or **Netiquette**, as it's called in Cyberspace. It's easy to come across as being rude when communicating over the Net, especially for the newbie (new user). However, a few rules of netiquette will help you get off to a good start.

Remember:

1. There is a human being on the other end, so don't forget to be nice.
2. Be clear in your message; it's easy to cause a misunderstanding.
3. Don't forget to add your name to the end of a message.
4. Keep your signature short.
5. Use a spell checker!
6. Don't send the same message out to multiple newsgroups and mailing lists. This is called **spamming** and it's despised on the Internet.
7. Don't engage in bitter online arguments. This is called **flaming**.
8. DON'T WRITE IN ALL-CAPITAL LETTERS LIKE THIS! This is called SHOUTING and it's irritating and hard to read.
9. Spend some time getting used to the discussion group before making your first posting.
10. Use descriptive titles in the subject line of all your postings.
11. When everything else fails, use common sense.

More on the subject of netiquette can be found at the ***Netiquette Home Page*** (**`http://www.fau.edu/rinaldi/netiquette.html`**).

Creating a Basic Web Page

"*We have done some work with the net, but what I find when I speak to other public school teachers is fear. They are afraid to get involved and try. It sounds strange coming from teachers, but that's the truth. However, in many cases I think the fear comes from lack of experience or exposure to the Internet. A large percentage of public school classrooms cannot afford the technology or training for teachers.*"

Lynore M. Carnuccio
Mustang Public Schools, Mustang, Oklahoma
nuch@flash.net

Okay, so now you've learned a lot about how to *use* the Web, but it's time to learn how to become a *part* of it by creating and publishing your own Web pages. Think you can't do it? Don't worry, it's really not very difficult—no more so than using a word processor. And with the right software, a bit of practice, and lots of patience, you and your students will be creating exciting Web pages in no time.

To get started, you need *only* two things: a basic text editor or word processor for *creating* the page, and a Web browser for *viewing* it.

Starting Up with HTML

The Web works magically because of a common language called **HTML**, which stands for HyperText Markup Language. HTML enables *all* Web browsers to display your page, even though users will be using a variety of different computer systems, such as Windows, Windows 95, or Macintosh.

HTML uses something called *tags*, which, among other things, change the format of what the Web page will look like.

Every Web page needs certain basic tags. Here are the steps for creating a simple Web page:

- You would create the file with an editor or word processing program. The bracketed tags are the source code; the text in italics is user input.

```
<HTML>
<HEAD>
<TITLE> My First Web Page </TITLE>
</HEAD>
```

```
<BODY>
This is my first step into the exciting realm of the World
Wide Web.
</BODY>
</HTML>
```

Tip: Tags can either be in uppercase, lowercase, or both. Use whatever you find more convenient.

- Here's the translation:

`<HTML> </HTML>`	These tags verify that this is indeed an HTML document. `<HTML>` comes at beginning of the document, and `</HTML>` comes at the end.
`<HEAD> </HEAD>`	These tags indicate the top or head of the Web document. They come before and after the `<TITLE>` tags.
`<TITLE> </TITLE>`	This is where you put the title of your Web page. The title will then appear on the menu bar at the top of the Web browser.
`<BODY> </BODY>`	This is where you place the contents of the actual document (i.e., text, links, graphics, etc.).

Tip: After creating your Web page in a text editor or word processor, give it a name, add an .html extension (e.g., `eslcafe.html`). and save it as a text file. Next, open your Web browser, choose Open File from the menu, and select your .html file. You'll then be able to view your newly created Web page. Each time you make some changes, though, don't forget to click on your Web browser's Reload button.

Doing More with HTML

You can jazz up your Web page by changing text size and font, experimenting with paragraphs and lines, adding links to other Web pages, adding color and background, and including pictures.

Text

For example, if you want to make your text **bold**, you need to surround the text with bold tags like this:

```
<B> </B>
```

For example,

```
<B> I love the Internet! </B>
```

I love the Internet!

<B> is where you want the bold text to begin, and </B> is where you want the bold text to end.

Or, if you want *italics*, you enclose italic tags like this:

```
<I> </I>
Dave is a <I> great </I> teacher!
```

Dave is a *great* teacher!

Easy, isn't it!

Heads

There are six levels of *header* tags that change the size of the text. <H1> is the largest and <H6> is the smallest.

```
<H1> Hello! </H1>
```

Hello!

```
<H6> Hello! </H6>
```

Hello!

You can also change the font size by using the *font* tag. Size ranges from 1–7, with 1 being the smallest and 7 the largest, as in:

```
<FONT SIZE=4> </FONT>
```

For example, `<FONT SIZE=4> Dave's ESL Cafe </FONT>`

Dave's ESL Cafe

As mentioned previously, there are tags that change the *style* of the text, such as:

Bold <B> </B>
Italic <I> </I>
Underlined <U> </U>
Blink (causes the text to blink) <BLINK> </BLINK>

Watch out: Blinking text can be quite annoying, so please use with caution.

Paragraphs and Lines

The <BR> tag ends a line without adding a line space, such as:

```
Welcome to....... <BR>
Dave's ESL Cafe
```

Welcome to.......
Dave's ESL Cafe

The <P> tag also ends a line, but adds a space, as in:

```
Welcome to........ <P>
Dave's ESL Cafe
```

Welcome to.......

Dave's ESL Cafe

The <HR> tag divides the page into sections:

```
Menu:
<HR>
ESL Graffiti Wall
<HR>
ESL Help Center
<HR>
ESL Idiom Page
<HR>
```

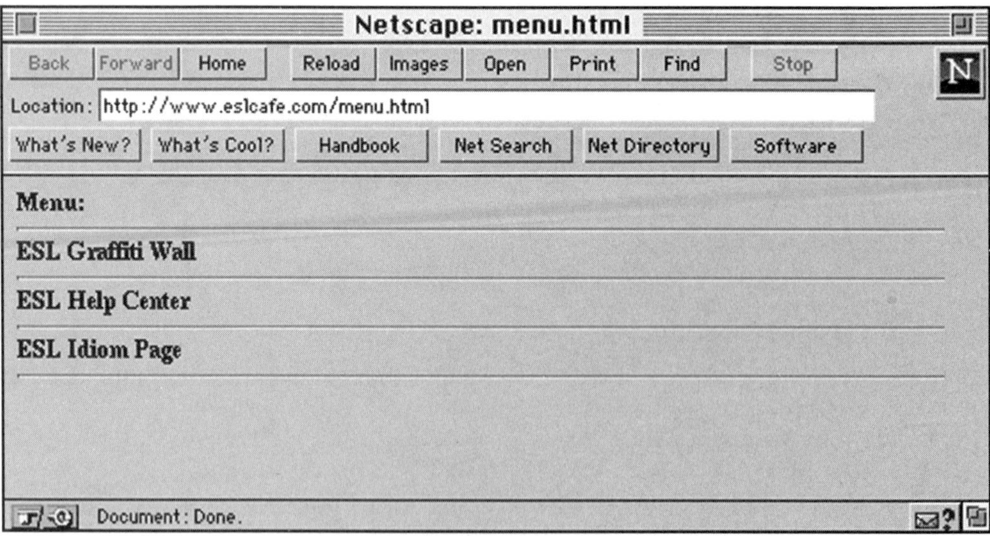

You probably want more than just plain text, so let's learn a few tricks to spice up your page.

Links

The *Link* tag enables you to add a hyperlink to other Web pages. Here's the tag:

```
<A HREF="URL">name-of-link</A>
```

A link to my home page looks like this:

```
<A HREF="http://www.eslcafe.com">Dave's ESL Cafe</A>
```

You may also want to include a link to your own e-mail address so that people can easily e-mail you from their Web browsers. Here's the tag:

```
<a href=mailto:e-mail-address>e-mail-address</a>
```

A link to my e-mail address looks like this:

```
<a href=mailto:sperling@eslcafe.com>sperling@eslcafe.com</a>
```

Tip: Check your HTML "grammar" at *Weblint* (**http://www.khoros.unm.edu/staff/neilb/weblint.html**).

Color and Background

You can add some color to your pages by changing the color of the background, text, and links. To do this, you'll need to add the hexadecimal numbers to your HTML document, which can be done automatically at **ColorMaker** (http://www.missouri.edu/~wwwtools/colormaker/).
For example, <BODY BGCOLOR="#FFFF00"> changes the background to a bright yellow color.

Another way to change the look and feel of your page is by adding a *background graphic* to your Web page. Here's the tag:

```
<Body Background="name-of-file">
```

For example,

```
<Body Background="Dave.GIF">
```

Remember: Most browsers recognize graphics in GIF or JPEG format (.GIF, .JPG, or .JPEG file extension). More help can be found at Yahoo's *Computers and Internet: Software:Graphics* (**http://www/yahoo.com/Computers_and_Internet/Software/Graphics/**).

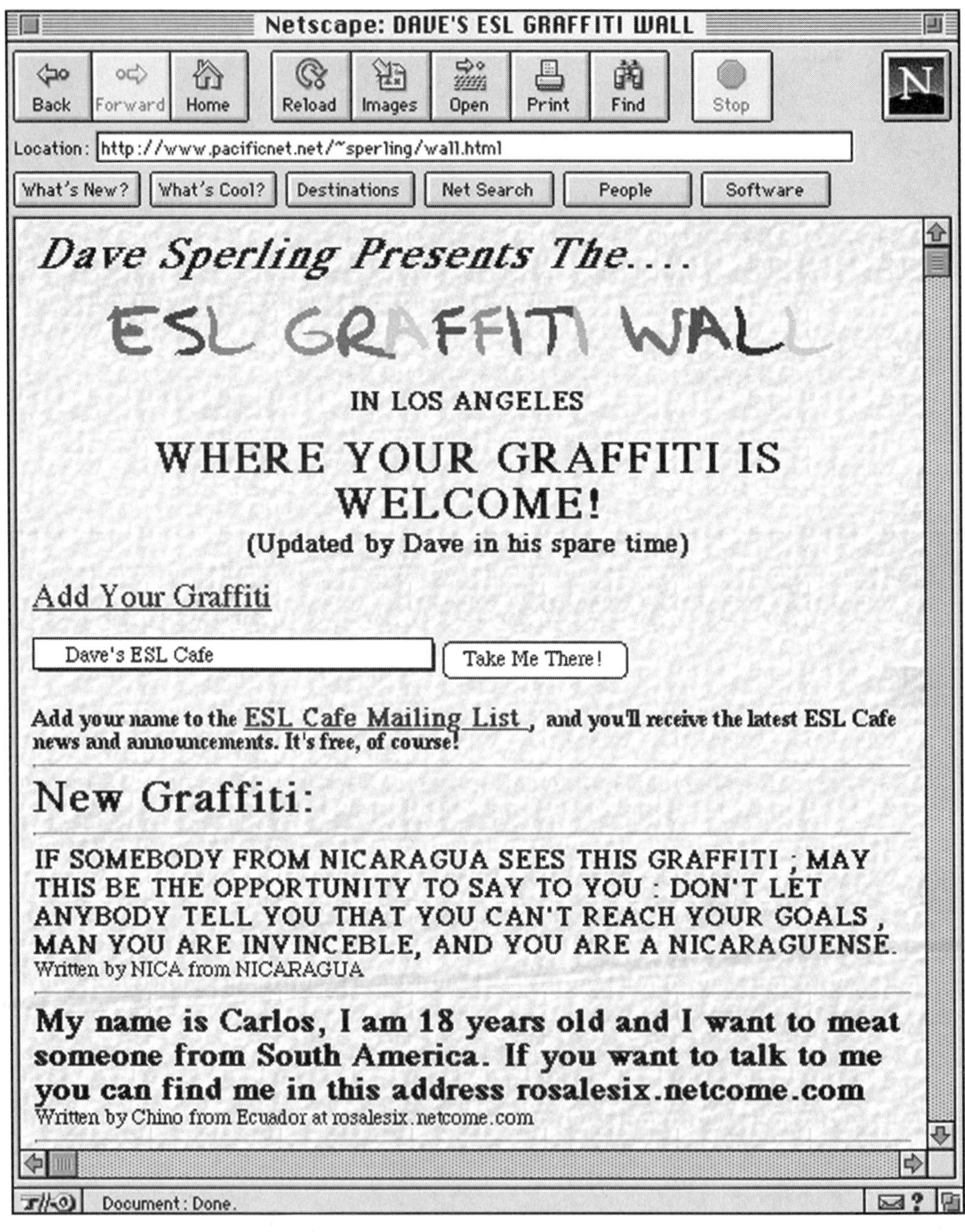
Netscape: DAVE'S ESL GRAFFITI WALL
Back
Forward
Home
Reload
Images
Open
Print
Find
Stop
Location: http://www.pacificnet.net/~sperling/wall.html
What's New?
What's Cool?
Destinations
Net Search
People
Software
Dave Sperling Presents The....
ESL GRAFFITI WALL
IN LOS ANGELES
WHERE YOUR GRAFFITI IS WELCOME!
(Updated by Dave in his spare time)
Add Your Graffiti
Dave's ESL Cafe
Take Me There!
Add your name to the ESL Cafe Mailing List, and you'll receive the latest ESL Cafe news and announcements. It's free, of course!
New Graffiti:
IF SOMEBODY FROM NICARAGUA SEES THIS GRAFFITI ; MAY THIS BE THE OPPORTUNITY TO SAY TO YOU : DON'T LET ANYBODY TELL YOU THAT YOU CAN'T REACH YOUR GOALS , MAN YOU ARE INVINCEBLE, AND YOU ARE A NICARAGUENSE.
Written by NICA from NICARAGUA
My name is Carlos, I am 18 years old and I want to meat someone from South America. If you want to talk to me you can find me in this address rosalesix.netcome.com
Written by Chino from Ecuador at rosalesix.netcome.com
Document: Done.

Tip: For a comprehensive listing of free background images, head over to Yahoo's *Backgrounds* (**http://www.yahoo.com/Computers_and_Internet/Internet/World_Wide_Web/Page_Design_and_Layout/Backgrounds/**).

Pictures

Icons and graphics are another good way to add some flavor to your Web page, and there's no shortage of high-quality graphics on the Internet—most of them free. **Yahoo's Icon page** is a good spot to begin your treasure hunt (http://www.yahoo.com/Computers_and_Internet/Internet/World_Wide_Web/Programming/Icons/); afterward head over to **Moby's Icon Archive** (http://www.dsv.su.se/~matti-hu/archive.html).

Tip: You can create a free professional custom logo for your Web page at the *Signboard Factory* (**http://madeira.cc.hokudai.ac.jp/RD/yamamoto/factory.html**). Highly recommended!

Common HTML Tags

Body	<BODY> </BODY>
Bold	<B> </B>
Break	
Center	<CENTER> </CENTER>
Head	<HEAD> </HEAD>
Heading - First	<H1> </H1>
Heading - Second	<H2> </H2>
Heading - Third	<H3> </H3>
Heading - Fourth	<H4> </H4>
Heading - Fifth	<H5> </H5>
Heading - Sixth	<H6> </H6>
Horizontal Rule	<HR>
HTML	<HTML> </HTML>
Images	<IMG SRC="image name">
Italic	<I> </I>
Link	<A HREF="file name">
Linked Graphic	<A HREF="link name"> <IMG SRC="graphic name">
Linked text	<A HREF="link name"texttolink</A>>
Paragraph	<P>
Title	<TITLE>

HTML Editors to the Rescue

HTML Editors simplify the process of generating complex Web pages by enabling you to create HTML documents in a word processing-like **WYSIWYG** (What You See Is What You Get) environment, automatically producing complicated tags for graphics, tables, forms, lists, and even frames. And the good news is that most of the editors are readily available on the Net for your downloading pleasure.

My current favorite is **Adobe's Pagemill** (for both Windows and Macintosh), which is very powerful and simple to use. You'll find support for frames, tables, text wrap, and alignment, as well as a built-in spell checker and an integrated source code editor. Download a free demo at their home page (`http://www.adobe.com/prodindex/ pagemill/main.html`).

Some other excellent alternatives include Netscape's very own **Navigator Gold 3.0** (`http://home.netscape.com/`), which is a combination browser and HTML editor; Microsoft's **FrontPage** (`http://www.microsoft.com/frontpage/`), a complete tool for creating, publishing, and managing your own Web site; and SoftQuad's **HoTMetaL Pro** (`http://www.sq.com/products/hotmetal/hmp-org.htm`), which is easy to use and accurate.

Other good choices include these for the Macintosh:

AOL Press
`(http://www.aolpress.com/press/index.html)`

HTML Editor
`(http://dragon.acadiau.ca/~giles/HTML_Editor/Documentation.html)`

Web Weaver
`(http://www.miracleinc.com/)`

and these for Windows:

AOL Press
`(http://www.aolpress.com/press/index.html)`

HotDog Web Editor
`(http://www.sausage.com/)`

HTML Assistant Pro
`(http://www.brooknorth.com/)`

Visual Web
`(http://www.vizweb.com/)`

Tip: You can also automatically create a Web page online at *Adgrafix* (**`http://www.adgrafix.com/cgi-bin/htmlfm.pl`**) and the *Homepage Creator System* (**`http://theinter.net/www/future21/create1.html`**).

Onto the Net

The final step is getting your Web page onto the Internet, and this is done by **uploading**, or transferring the files from your own personal computer, onto the computer where your Internet account is located. If you have a PPP/SLIP or dedicated connection, this can easily be accomplished by using an FTP utility, such as **Fetch** (`http://www.dartmouth.edu/pages/softdev/fetch.html`) for Macintosh, or **CuteFTP** (`http://www.cuteftp.com/`) for Windows.

Promoting Your Web Page

Okay, now you've created this fantastic Web page, but how are you going to get the world to visit? Try:

- E-mailing every friend you've made on the Internet!
- Writing to appropriate Web sites and asking for a link.
- Announcing it on appropriate mailing lists.
- Using free announcing services. The best are **Promote It** (`http://www.iTools.com/promote-it/`), which has links to just about every possible source on the Net to promote your Web page, and **Submit It** (`http://204.57.42.244/submit.htm`), which is probably the single best place to begin your Web promotion: fill out a single form and Submit It! automatically submits the information to 18 of the world's major search engines and directories.

Tip: Set up a counter so that you can keep track of the number of visitors to your page. For a hassle-free counter, try *Web Counter* (**`http://www.digits.com`**).

Learning More

I've only touched upon some of the very basics of HTML and the world of Web page construction. Have I whetted your appetite? I hope so! To continue your journey, visit NCSA's **Beginners Guide to HTML** (`http://www.ncsa.uiuc.edu/General/Internet/WWW/HTMLPrimer.html`), which is one of the best HTML introductions available anywhere on the Internet.

Dave's Guide to the Best of the Web

"*Because the possibilities are endless, I am always able to improve my ability to teach by offering students activities that can take them almost anywhere in the world right from our school in Austin.*"

Kim Gray
Associate Director, IELS Language School
Austin, Texas

"*This computer has changed my life.*"

Annette Scherr
Sylmar High School, California
ascherr@lausd.k12.ca.us

Categories

Articles
Associations
Bilingual Education
Bookstores on the Web
Business English
Computer Assisted Language Learning (CALL)
Conferences
Dictionaries
Disabilities
Distance Education
Drama
Electronic ESL/EFL Publications
Encyclopedias
English for Specific Purposes (ESP)
Games
Grammar
Lesson Plans and Material
Libraries
Linguistics
Links
Listening and Speaking
Literacy
Literature
Magazines
Meeting Other Teachers
Movies and Screenplays
Multicultural Issues
News and Newspapers
Online Help
Poetry
Pronunciation
Proverbs and Quotations
Public Speaking
Publishers
Quizzes
Resources
School Directories
Schools—Individual ESL/EFL Programs
Songs and Music
Student Internet Projects
Teacher Training
Testing and Assessment
Theatre and Drama
TOEFL
Tongue Twisters
U.S. Immigration
Video
Vocabulary, Idioms, and Slang
Writing

Articles

Articles
(http://ietn.snunit.k12.il/articles.htm)
Lots of links from the Israeli English Teachers Network.

BenJX: Language Learning
(http://www.ozemail.com.au/~cdug/)
Articles that give "practical hints and suggestions for learning and teaching any language quickly."

CARL UnCover
(http://www.carl.org/uncover/unchome.html)
CARL UnCover is an online article delivery service, a table of contents database, and a keyword index to nearly 17,000 periodicals.

Comparison of Two Web Sites, "Ex*change" and "Dave's ESL Cafe on the Web"
(http://humanum.arts.cuhk.hk/~cmc/tech-mania/ann1.htm)
The Chinese University of Hong Kong compares and contrasts two popular ESL Web sites, Ex*change and Dave's ESL Cafe.

The Development of ESL Collocational Knowledge
(http://www.cltr.uq.oz.au:8000/users/christina.gitsaki/thesis/contents.html)
The completed graduate thesis of Christina Gitsaki.

Directory of MA Dissertations
(http://www.surrey.ac.uk/ELI/thesis.html)
Directory of dissertations written by students of the English Language Institute at the University of Surrey.

E-Mail Keypals for Language Fluency
(http://www.kyoto-su.ac.jp/people/teacher/trobb/keypals.html)
Thomas N. Robb's article published in the newsletter of the Foreign Language Educators of New Jersey.

History of the English Language
(http://ebbs.english.vt.edu/hel/hel.html)
Everything you ever wanted to know about the history of English, with several excellent links. Don't forget to join their mailing list, HEL-L.

The Internet as an Educational Tool in ESOL Writing Instruction
(http://thecity.sfsu.edu/~funweb/thesis.htm)
M.A. thesis from Internet great, Karla Frizler.

Language Professional's Guide to the World Wide Web
(http://agoralang.com/calico/webarticle.html)
Carolyn G. Fidelman's informative article, published by the *CALICO Journal*.

Links to ESL/EFL Articles on the Net
(http://www.aitech.ac.jp/~iteslj/Links/ArticleLinks.html)
The *Internet TESL Journal's* astounding collection of links to ESL/EFL articles available on the Web. Highly recommended!

Teaching English to Japanese Students
(http://humanities.byu.edu/elc/Teacher/BasicHandbook/JapaneseStudents)
Informative article written by Miki Ikeda.

TESOL Journal and TESOL Quarterly: Selected Articles
(http://www.ncbe.gwu.edu/miscpubs/tesol)
Full-text articles from the *TESOL Journal* and *TESOL Quarterly.*

Associations

The American Association of Intensive English Programs
(http://www.outfitters.com/com/aaiep/)
An organization of intensive English programs presented by their directors.

The Association of Language Testers in Europe (ALTE)
(http://www.edunet.com/alte/)
European association of providers of language examinations.

Australian Technology Enhanced Language Learning (ATELL)
(http://www.arts.unimelb.edu.au:80/Horwood/ATELL/atell.html)
Association of language centers located in Australia.

The British Association for Applied Linguistics
(http://www.swan.ac.uk/cals/baal.html)
A professional association based in the U.K., which provides a forum for people interested in language and the applications of linguistics.

The British Council
(http://www.britcoun.org/)
The British Council promotes a wider knowledge of the United Kingdom and the English language.

California Association of Teachers of English to Speakers of Other Languages (CATESOL)
(http://www.crl.com/~malarak/catesol/catesol.html)
An organization dedicated to the support of English as a Second Language teachers throughout both California and Nevada.

Canada TESOL
(http://www.tesl.ca)

Central States Conference on the Teaching of Foreign Languages
(http://www.iupui.edu/~cscfl/)
An association of some 1,800 foreign language teachers from Arkansas, Colorado, Illinois, Indiana, Iowa, Kansas, Kentucky, Michigan, Minnesota, Missouri, Nebraska, North Dakota, Ohio, Oklahoma, South Dakota, Tennessee, and Wisconsin.

The Computer Assisted Language Instruction Consortium (CALICO)
(http://calico.org/)
A professional organization of members interested in both education and high technology.

ConnTESOL
(http://www.mindport.net/~goldstei/cttesol.html)
Connecticut Teachers of English to Speakers of Other Languages.

English Language Education Association in Turkey
(http://www.bilkent.edu.tr/prv/bilkent-cwis/elea/elea.html)
The English Language Education Association in Turkey.

France TESOL
(http://www.wfi.fr/tesol/home.html)
Association representing the interests of EFL professionals in France.

Global Schoolnet Foundations
(http://www.gsn.org)
One of the leaders in the instructional applications of telecommunications.

International Association for Learning Laboratories (IALL)
(http://eleazar.dartmouth.edu/IALL/)
Dedicated to the promotion of language learning with technology.

International Association of Teachers of English as a Foreign Language (IATEFL)
(http://www.man.ac.uk/IATEFL/)
An international organization meeting the professional needs of teachers of English as a foreign language.

International Society for Technology in Education
(http://isteonline.uoregon.edu/)
A nonprofit professional organization dedicated to the improvement of education through computer-based technology.

Japan Association of Language Teaching (JALT)
(http://langue.hyper.chubu.ac.jp/jalt)
The official JALT home page is packed with excellent resources and information.

Korea TESOL
(http://www.ncmc.cc.mi.us:443/esl/)
Korea's TESOL association.

Language Laboratory Association of Japan
(http://langue.hyper.chubu.ac.jp/lla/)
An organization interested in research in using technology as a means for raising the efficiency of foreign language education.

MATSDA Materials Development Association
(http://cis.nmclites.edu/~banfi/MATSDA.html)
An association promoting innovation and quality in L2 language materials development by bringing together teachers, researchers, writers, and publishers.

Michigan TESOL
(http://polyglot.cal.msu.edu/mitesol/)
Michigan Teachers of English to Speakers of Other Languages.

National Council of Teachers of English (NCTE)
(http://www.ncte.org/)
With over 90,000 members, the National Council of Teachers of English works on improving the teaching of English and the language arts at all levels of education.

Ontario TESL
(http://www.vaxxine.com/teslont)
An affiliate of TESL Canada.

Spain TESOL
(http://www.eire/ink.com/tesol-sp/)
Nationwide organization of English language teachers in Spain.

TESOL
(http://www.tesol.edu/)
Home page to the one and only TESOL, with almost 18,000 members worldwide.

TESOL Ukraine
(http://www.ah.kiev.ua/efl/tesolhom.html)
Information on workshops, seminars and summer institutes from TESOL Ukraine.

Thai TESOL
(http://www.nectec.or.th/users/ttesol/index.html)
Professional development of teachers of English in Thailand.

Writing and Computers Association
(http://www.cogs.susx.ac.uk/users/mike/wa/wricom.html)
An association that promotes communication between individuals and groups with an interest in the writing process and in computer support for writing.

Bilingual Education

Bilingual Education Resources on the Net
(http://www.estrellita.com/~karenm/bil.html)
Collection of resources from Karen Myer, author of *Estrellita Accelerated Beginning Spanish Reading.*

Bilingual Education
(http://www.csun.edu/~hcedu013/eslbil.html)
Collection of links from Dr. Martin Levine of California State University, Northridge.

Bilingual ESL Network (BEN)
(http://tism.bevc.blacksburg.va.us/BEN.html)
Edwin Nieves's valuable resource includes material and discussion. BEN can also create a Web page for your class or program. Highly recommended!

Washington State University's Bilingual Education and ESL Resources
(http://www.educ.wsu.edu:80/esl/index.html)
Includes a launch pad, an archive of computer-assisted, language-learning activity plans, and a list of other resources.

Bookstores on the Web

Blackwell's Bookshops
(http://www.blackwell.co.uk/bookshops/)
Direct from Oxford, England, you can purchase books online from the "world's finest academic bookseller."

Booklink
(http://www.intac.com/~booklink/)
Online bookstore that specializes in ESL/EFL and multicultural books.

The ESL Cafe Bookstore
(http://www/eslcafe.com/bookstore)
Dave's ESL Cafe, in association with Amazon.Com, offers the largest selection of ESL material available on the Net at discounted prices.

ESL Network
(http://www.esl.net/)
Another fine example of online shopping for language learning and ESL materials.

International Student Bookshop
(http://www.ilcgroup.com/books)
Specialists in English language teaching books and materials.

Virtual Bookshop
(http://www.u-net.com/eflweb/b-shop.htm)
Virtual ESL bookshop brought to you by ESLWeb.

Business English

Business Meetings
(http://www.stir.ac.uk/epd/higdox/Vallance/Diss/fp.htm)
Site devoted to developing the skills required to participate in business meetings.

Computer Assisted Language Learning (CALL)

Athelstan ONLINE
(http://www.nol.net/~athel/athel.html)
Lots of resources and demo software from Athelstan, publisher and distributor of products related to technology and second language learning.

CALL Cookbook
(http://www.owlnet.rice.edu/~ling417/)
A student project from Rice University, the CALL Cookbook provides "inspirational examples ('recipes') of working, web-based activities we created to add flavor to the regular meat-and-potatoes classroom study of a foreign language."

CALL Electronic Journal
(http://www.lc.tut.ac.jp/callej/callej.html)
Electronic publication from the Japan Association of Language Teaching (JALT).

Computer Assisted Language Learning
(http://www.chorus.cycor.ca/Duber/call.html)
One of the very best CALL resources available, from the talented Jim Duber.

Computer Assisted Language Learning Web Board
(http://www.eslcafe.com/discussion/wwwboard8/wwwboard.html)
Interactive discussion board for teachers interested in CALL.

Computer-Mediated Communication in Foreign Language Education: An Annotated Bibliography
(http://www.lll.hawaii.edu/nflrc/NetWorks/NW3/)
Very comprehensive bibliography on computer technology and its applications in second language teaching.

Cutting Edge CALL Resources
(http://www.chorus.cycor.ca/Duber/m004d.html)
More interactive creations from Jim Duber.

Ohio University CALL Lab
(http://www.tcom.ohiou.edu/OU_Language/OU_Language.html)
First-rate resource from John McVicker.

Conferences

Conferences
(http://www.hut.fi/~rvilmi/Conference/)
Ruth Vilmi's list of conferences past, present, and future.

TESL-L Conference List
(gopher://CUNYVM.CUNY.EDU:70/00/Subject%20Specific%20Gophers/teslfl/Teaching%20English%20as%20a%20Foreign%20Language%20-%20The%20Profession/Conferences)
Very comprehensive listing of conferences from TESL-L.

VOLTERRE-FR's Conference Announcements Worldwide
(http://www.wfi.fr/volterre/confw.html)
From one of the great ESL/EFL Web sites in the world, VOLTERRE-FR.

Dictionaries

The Alternative English Dictionary
(http://www.notam.uio.no/~hcholm/altlang/ht/English.html)
Encyclopedic collection of English slang.

Australiana
(http://www.ozemail.com.au/~davesag/auzzie.html)
An insight into Australian slang, written by Dave Sag.

Biotechnology Dictionary
(http://biotech.chem.indiana.edu/pages/dictionary.html)
An illustrated glossary that contains terms associated with genetics and biochemistry, as well as general biology, chemistry, pharmacology, toxicology, and medicine.

BritSpeak
(http://pages.prodigy.com/NY/NYC/britspk/main.html)
"Bilingual" dictionary for both British -> American or American -> British English.

Dictionary of Occupational Titles
(http://www.wave.net/upg/immigration/dot_index.html)
A listing of thousands of job titles.

Hypertext Webster Interface
(http://c.gp.cs.cmu.edu:5103/prog/webster)
Look up a word and you'll get the definition in seconds.

The Internet Language Dictionary
(http://www.netlingo.com/)
A comprehensive listing of new vocabulary from the World Wide Web.

Kev's Down-Under Dictionary
(http://wilson.com.au/diction.html)
Another terrific source for Australian slang.

List of Dictionaries
(http://math-www.uni-paderborn.de/HTML/Dictionaries.html)
One of the best collections of links to dictionaries from all over the world.

New Zealand English to U.S. English Dictionary
(http://nz.com/NZ/Culture/NZDic.html)
A good place to brush up on your Kiwi English.

The Notable Citizens of Planet Earth Biographical Dictionary
(http://www.tiac.net/users/parallax/)
Biographical information on over 18,000 people from ancient times to the present day.

On-line Dictionaries
(http://www.bucknell.edu/~rbeard/diction.html)
A list of online dictionaries and thesauri for linguists and other writers.

Roget's Thesaurus
(http://humanities.uchicago.edu/forms_unrest/ROGET.html)
Online version of this timeless classic.

The Totally Unofficial Rap Dictionary
(http://www.sci.kun.nl/thalia/rapdict/)
For students who like rap music.

WWWebster Dictionary
(http://www.m-w.com/dictionary)
From Merriam-Webster, searches include pronunciation, etymology, and a built-in thesaurus. Probably the very best English dictionary on the Web. Highly recommended!

Disabilities

The Braille Forum
(http://www.acb.org/Magazine/)
Some good information on teaching blind students.

Deaf/Hard of Hearing
(http://sage.und.nodak.edu/dept/dss/hearing.htm)
Help for teachers working with the deaf or hard of hearing.

Kennedy Center Home Page
(http://kc.gpct.vanderbilt.edu/)
Helpful tips for parents, teachers, and others who work with children and adults with disabilities.

WebABLE!
(http://www.webable.com/)
A repository for people with disabilities.

Distance Education

Distance Education Clearinghouse
(http://www.uwex.edu/disted/home.html)
Information and resources from the University of Wisconsin–Extension.

Distance Education Resource Page
(http://www.ola.bc.ca/ola/library/inetresources/distedlinks.html)
Superb resource from the Open Learning Agency.

Distance Learning in Finland
(http://www.hut.fi/~rvilmi/OFDL/)
Terrific information on distance learning from Ruth Vilmi.

Distance Learning Programs
(http://www.wfi.fr/volterre/distancelearning.html)
Several distance programs for graduate studies in TESL.

Globewide Network Academy Course Catalog
(http://www.gnacademy.org/uu-gna/documents/catalog/index.html)
An educational and research organization dedicated to providing a "competitive marketplace online for distance learning courses and programs."

The University of Michigan Distance Education Archives
(http://www.outreach.umich.edu/pages/de_page.html)
Archive of citations and abstracts from the Education Resources Information Center (ERIC), the world's largest educational database.

The World Lecture Hall
(http://wwwhost.cc.utexas.edu/world/instruction/index.html)
Amazing collection of links to pages created by teachers from around the world who are using the Web to furnish class materials. Highly recommended!

Drama

Shakespeare Eclectic Fiction Interactive Theatre
(http://rpg.net/larp/)
Interactive drama, freeform live action role play, and interactive theatre.

Electronic ESL/EFL Publications

EFLWeb
(http://www.u-net.com/eflweb/)
An online magazine for those teaching and learning English as a Foreign Language.

English Teachers' Electronic Newsletter
(http://ietn.snunit.k12.il/newslett.htm)
Issues have included information on reading, writing, testing, and Computer Assisted Language Learning (CALL).

Exchange
(http://deil.lang.uiuc.edu/exchange/)
Publishes writings of non-native English speakers from all over the world and provides English self-study materials.

Headway—Ideas and Comments for Teachers of English
(http://www1.oup.co.uk/oup/elt/headway?)
Ideas and comments for teachers of English in an online magazine, published by Oxford University Press.

Heinemann ELT—First Class Newsletter
(http://www.heinemann.co.uk/heinemann/elt/1stclass/first.html)
Includes teaching tips and free photocopiable activities.

Impact! Online
(http://www.ed.uiuc.edu/impact/)
A hypertextual newsreader for intermediate and advanced learners of English as a Second or Foreign Language.

Internet TESL Journal
(http://www.aitech.ac.jp/~iteslj/)
This fine monthly web magazines includes articles, research papers, lesson plans, classroom handouts, teaching ideas, and links. Not to be missed!

iT's On-Line
(http://its-online.com/)
Excellent ESL Web magazine for both students and teachers.

Kairos: A Journal For Teachers of Writing in Webbed Environments
(http://english.ttu.edu/kairos/)
Published three times a year, Kairos deals "specifically with the challenges of writing in hypertextual environments, primarily (but not solely) the World Wide Web." Super resource for writing teachers.

The Language Teacher Online
(http://langue.hyper.chubu.ac.jp/jalt/pub/tlt)
You'll find excerpts from *The Language Teacher*, the monthly publication of the Japan Association for Language Teaching (JALT).

Soon Online Magazine
(http://www.soon.org.uk/)
New magazine for students learning English.

The TESL Electronic Journal, TESL-EJ
(http://violet.berkeley.edu/~cwp/TESL-EJ/index.html)
Includes articles, reviews, and conference information.

Wings Electronic Magazine
(http://weber.u.washington.edu/~wings/wings.html)
Published for and by students involved in Latrobe University's International Student Lists project.

Write Away
(http://137.111.169.8:80/writeaway/)
A showcase of writing by adult migrants in Australia. Not to be missed!

Encyclopedias

Bartlett's Familiar Quotations
(http://www.cc.columbia.edu/acis/bartleby/bartlett/)
Online version of the original 1901 classic by John Bartlett.

Britannica Online
(http://www.eb.com:195/bol/)
One of the best, but not free ($14.95 per month).

Encyclopaedia of the Orient
(http://www.i-cias.com/e.o/index.htm)
Specializes in North Africa and the Middle East.

Encyclopedia Mystica
(http://www.pantheon.org/myth)
An encyclopedia on mythology, folklore, mysticism, and more.

International Financial Encyclopaedia
(http://www.euro.net/innovation/Finance_Base/Fin_encyc.html)
The world's only interactive financial encyclopaedia.

English for Specific Purposes (ESP)

English for Science and Technology
(http://www.hut.fi/~rvilmi/EST/)
Ruth Vilmi's page of excellent links to science and technology resources.

English for Specific Purposes
(http://www.eslcafe.com/discussion/wwwboard9/wwwboard.html)
ESL Cafe's discussion forum on English for specific purposes.

International Directory of Professionals in ESP
(http://www.u-aizu.ac.jp/~t-orr/international-esp-menu.html)
Maintained by Thomas Orr; you'll find a directory of names and contact information of ESP professionals around the world.

Resources for Teachers of English for Science and Technology
(http://www.cibnor.conacyt.mx/est/est.html)
This excellent resource from Roy Bowers is also mirrored in Mexico, France, and Hong Kong.

Topics in Medical English
(http://www.interserver.miyazaki-med.ac.JP/~Kimball/med/1.html)
Compiled by Professor John Kimball of Miyazaki Medical College; topics include the Heart, Nutrition, Sensory Anatomy, and Skeletal and Orthopedic Anatomy.

Games

American Crossword Puzzle
(http://AmericanPresident.com/xword.html)
Online crossword puzzle on the American presidents.

Anagram Insanity
(http://infobahn.com/pages/anagram.html)
An anagram is a word or phrase made by scrambling the letters in another word or phrase, and here is a place that does it for you automatically. Very cool!

Cobuild Definitions Game
(http://titania.cobuild.collins.co.uk/defsgameform.html)
Click on a button to get a randomly selected definition from the *Cobuild Dictionary*. Afterwards, students can try to guess the word being defined. Lots of fun!

Fake out!
(http://www.hmco.com/hmco/school/dictionary/)
Choose a word and guess its definition. Grades include K–2, 3–5, and 6 and above. Kids can also write their own fake definitions.

Gigabox
(http://www.dtd.com/)
Games include MindSports, Two Minute Warning, Bullpen, Herspace, and Dr. Fellowbug's Laboratory of Fun and Horror. Very creative site!

Inigo Gets Out
(http://darkwing.uoregon.edu/~leslieob/Inigo.ex.html)
Leslie Opp-Beckman's paper on mouse practice for ESL/EFL students; uses Amanda Goodenough's "Inigo Gets Out."

Interactive WWW Games
(http://einstein.et.tudelft.nl/~mvdlaan/texts/www_games.html)
Links to interactive games found on the Web. Includes TicTacToe, Hangman, Othello, and even Blackjack. Highly addictive!

John's Word Search Puzzles
(http://www.neosoft.com/~jrpotter/puzzles.html)
John Potter's collection of printable word search puzzles. Super resource!

The Palindrome Home Page
(http://www.ecst.csuchico.edu/~nanci/Pdromes/)
So what's a palindrome? A palindrome is a word or sentence that reads the same forward as it does backward, and this is a home page devoted exclusively to palindromes.

Searching for China: A WebQuest
(http://www.kn.pacbell.com/wired/China/ChinaQuest.html)
An amazing project from Pacific Bell where students can work together to create a special report, while at the same time trying to make sense out of a complex country called China.

Syndicate.com
(http://syndicate.com/)
Entertaining collection of puzzles, comic strips, word games, and more.

TESOL Game Paradise
(http://www.rede.com/eslgames/)
Collection of fun links from Everglory Publishing Company

Wacky Web Tales
(http://www.hmco.com/hmco/school/tales/index.html)
Good selection and lots of fun; students can create their own stories by filling in the blanks to The Mummy, The Camping Trip, and The Box.

Where's That From?
(http://www.intuitive.com:80/origins/)
Interactive game for guessing the origins of English words.

Grammar

Elements of Style, by William Strunk
(http://www.columbia.edu/acis/bartleby/strunk/)
Online version of this classic text from 1918.

Eleven Rules of Grammar
(http://www.concentric.net/~rag/grammar.htm)
Rules for avoiding some of the most common grammatical errors, created by Robert Giaquinta.

English Grammar FAQ, from alt.usage.english
(http://www.ling.lsa.umich.edu/jlawler/aue.html)
Postings from Linguistics professor John Lawler.

English Grammar Links for ESL Students
(http://www.gl.umbc.edu/~kpokoy1/grammar1.htm)
Good selection of links from Karen M. Hartman of the University of Maryland, Baltimore County.

ESL Help Center
(http://www.pacificnet.net/~sperling/wwwboard2/wwwboard.html)
Twenty-four-hour help for ESL/EFL students from an international team of ESL/EFL teachers. Don't miss it!

Gender-free Pronoun FAQ
(http://www.eecis.udel.edu/~chao/gfp/)
A general information source about gender-free alternatives to gendered pronouns, written by John Chao.

Grammar and Style Notes
(http://www.english.upenn.edu/~jlynch/Grammar/)
Jack Lynch's grammar and style guide.

Grammar Help
(http://www.hut.fi/~rvilmi/help/grammar_help/)
Hints, rules, and exercises on English grammar from Ruth Vilmi. Highly recommended!

LinguaCenter's Grammar Safari
(http://deil.lang.uiuc.edu/web.pages/grammarsafari.html)
A great place for students to gather real grammar examples found on the World Wide Web. Highly recommended!

On-line English Grammar
(http://www.edunet.com/english/grammar/toc.html)
Magnificent resource by Anthony Hughes. Don't miss it!

Netscape: The LinguaCenter Grammar Safari
Back
Forward
Home
Reload
Images
Open
Print
Find
Stop
Location: http://deil.lang.uiuc.edu/web.pages/grammarsafari.html
What's New?
What's Cool?
Handbook
Net Search
Net Directory
Software
DEIL /IEI
LinguaCenter
UIUC
Welcome to Grammar Safari
Document: Done.

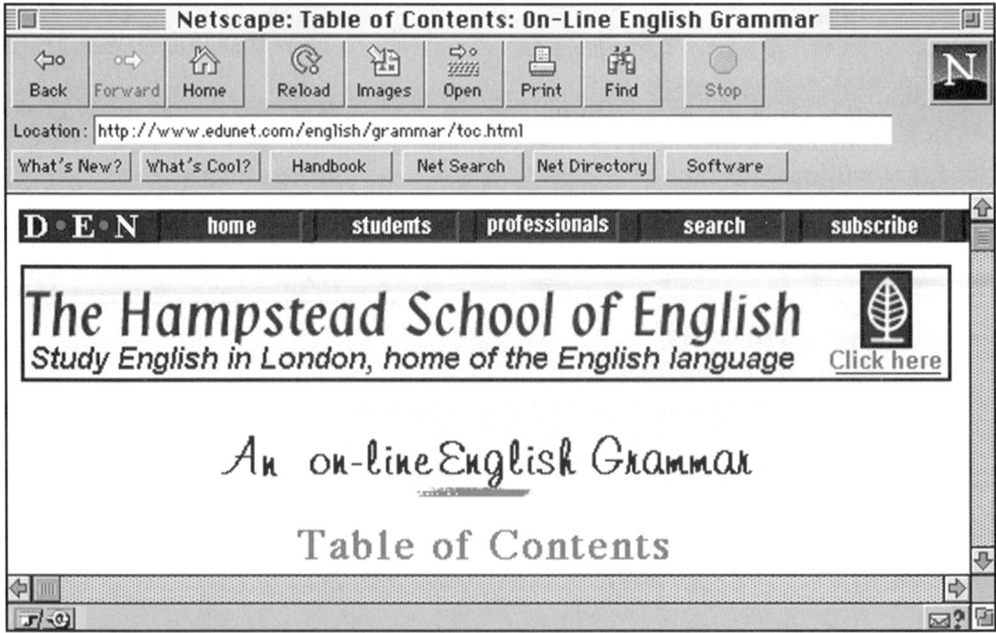
Netscape: Table of Contents: On-Line English Grammar
Back
Forward
Home
Reload
Images
Open
Print
Find
Stop
Location: http://www.edunet.com/english/grammar/toc.html
What's New?
What's Cool?
Handbook
Net Search
Net Directory
Software
D•E•N
home
students
professionals
search
subscribe
The Hampstead School of English
Study English in London, home of the English language
Click here
An on-line English Grammar
Table of Contents

Lesson Plans and Material

AskERIC Lesson Plans
(http://ericir.syr.edu/Virtual/Lessons/)
Free lesson plans, materials, and curriculums from ERIC.

Bilingual Lesson Plans for Grade K
(http://gopher.sedl.org/scimath/pasopartners/pphome. html)
English and Spanish material includes Five Senses, Spiders, and Dinosaurs.

Blue Web'n Applications Library from Pacific Bell
(http://www.kn.pacbell.com/wired/bluewebn/)
Lessons, activities, projects, resources, references, and tools, brought to you by Pacific Bell.

English Language Teaching
(http://www.stir.ac.uk/epd/higdox/stephen/elt.htm)
Stephen Luscombe's collection of poems, folk tales, and even an online phonology course.

English Teaching/Learning Materials
(http://www.ling.lancs.ac.uk/staff/visitors/kenji/kitao/material.htm)
Excellent collection from the Kitaos, including Holidays, Colonial Days, Communicating with Americans, and Developing Reading Strategy.

ESL Activities and Games
(http://www.eslcafe.com/discussion/wwwboard7/wwwboard.html)
Discussion forum on ESL/EFL activities and games.

ESL Idea Page
(http://www.pacificnet.net/~sperling/ideas.html)
A place where English language students and teachers throughout the world can brainstorm on ways to learn/teach English.

ESL Lessons from WSU
(http://www.educ.wsu.edu:80/esl/lessons.html)
(http://www.educ.wsu.edu:80/esl/content.html)
Material includes Bolivian Instruments, Glaciers, Lesson on Weather, Folk Song Lesson, Environment Lesson, and Easy Recipes.

ESL Lesson Plans
(http://www.csun.edu/~hcedu013/eslplans.html)
Collection of links from Dr. Martin Levine of California State University, Northridge.

ESL Quiz Center
(http://www.pacificnet.net/~sperling/quiz)
Students can take interactive quizzes on a broad range of categories that includes current news, geography, grammar, history, idioms, slang, words, people, reading comprehension, science, vocabulary, world culture, and writing. Answers are automatically checked in seconds.

ESL Teacher Connection
(http://www.sils.umich.edu/~jarmour/etc/etchome.html)
An open forum where teachers of English as a Second Language can share their own successful class activities and lesson plans with other teachers.

ESL Teaching-Learning Material
(http://www.eslcafe.com/discussion/wwwboard11/wwwboard.html)
Interactive forum on ESL teaching/learning material.

Heinemann English Language Teaching
(http://www.heinemann.co.uk/heinemann/elt/index.html)
Free photocopiable activities, idioms, and teacher tips are just some of the excellent free resources from Heinemann.

Gessler Teacher Tips
(http://www.gessler.com/gessler/teach.html)
Fun and interesting teaching tips from Gessler Publishing.

Great Ideas and Lessons that Work
(http://odin.cc.pdx.edu/~psu05592/activity.html)
Jane Welp's page full of helpful ideas.

Holidays
(http://www.capecod.net/Wixon/holidays.htm)
From the fine collection of Kathy Schrock.

Ideas and Lesson Plans for Writing Assignments
(http://www.ecnet.net/users/uwwwelp/topics.htm)
Tips from the English Language program at Northeastern Illinois University.

Internet TESL Journal
(http://www.aitech.ac.jp/~iteslj/)
Articles, research papers, lesson plans, classroom handouts, teaching ideas, and links.

John and Sarah's TEFL Pitstop
(http://www.classicweb.com/usr/jseng/jstefl.htm)
Growing collection of free TEFL classroom material.

K–12 Lesson Plans
(http://teams.lacoe.edu/documentation/places/lessons.html)
Links to lesson plans in all subjects, from the Los Angeles County Office of Education.

Lesson Plans and Resources for ESL, Bilingual, and Foreign Language Teachers
(http://www.csun.edu/~hcedu013/eslindex.html)
Another terrific resource from Dr. Martin Levine of California State University, Northridge.

Lingua@NET
(http://ncet.csv.warwick.ac.uk/WWW/temps/linguanet/)
Information and material for language teachers and learners.

Links to ESL Lessons on the Net
(http://www.aitech.ac.jp/~iteslj/Links/LessonLinks.html)
Super resource from the Internet TESL Journal.

PedagoNet
(http://www.pedagonet.com/)
Large and interesting database of learning material and resources.

Photocopiable Worksheets
(http://www.heinemann.co.uk/heinemann/elt/resource/wksht.html)
Samples of photocopiable resources produced by Heinemann ELT.

Pizzaz
(http://darkwing.uoregon.edu/~leslieob/pizzaz.html)
For people interested in "Zippy and Zany Zcribbling." Sections include Poetry, Fiction, Bag of Tricks, More Publishing Opportunities, and Other Teacher Resources. A wonderful gift from Leslie Opp-Beckman.

Purdue University On-line Writing Lab Handouts
(http://owl.trc.purdue.edu/by-topic.html)
Sections include Punctuation, Sentence Concerns, Parts of Speech, Research Paper Writing, Spelling, ESL, General Writing Concerns, Resumes, and Business/Professional Writing. Not to be missed!

Schoolhouse
(http://teacherpathfinder.syr.edu/Schoolhouse/)
Large collection of educational resources, projects, discussions, interactions, orations, lessons, curriculums, and standards for grades K–12.

Teachnet.com Lesson Ideas
(http://www.teachnet.com/lesson.html)
Lots of lesson ideas from Teachernet.com.

Libraries

Carrie
(http://www.ukans.edu/carrie/carrie_main.html)
A full-text electronic library.

The Electronic Library
(http://www.elibrary.com)
Full-text search of more than 150 full-text newspapers, nearly 800 full-text magazines, 2 international newswires, 2,000 classic books, hundreds of maps, thousands of photographs, as well as major works of literature and art. Free trial, but after that it's $9.95 a month for unlimited access.

The Internet Public Library
(http://ipl.sils.umich.edu/)
Divisions include Reference, Teen, Youth, and MOO. Rooms include Classroom, Exhibit Hall, and Reading Room.

The Library of Congress
(http://www.loc.gov)
A wondrous place packed with databases, resources, and information. Plan several visits!

National Library of Canada
(http://www.nlc-bnc.ca/)
The National Library of Canada (NLC) "gathers, makes known, preserves and promotes Canada's published heritage."

The On-Line Books Page
(http://www.cs.cmu.edu/Web/books.html)
Full text of over 2,100 English titles.

Linguistics

Constructed Human Languages
(http://www.quetzal.com/conlang.html)
Links and information on man-made human languages.

Ethnologue Database
(http://www-ala.doc.ic.ac.uk/~rap/Ethnologue/)
Information on some 6,500 languages spoken in the world, including alternate names, number of speakers, location, dialects, linguistic affiliation, and other sociolinguistic and demographic data. Highly recommended!

Human Language Page
(http://www.June29.com/HLP)
A comprehensive catalog of language-related Internet resources, including online language lessons, translating dictionaries, programs to help you study a language, and more.

Linguistics Resources on the Internet
(http://www.sil.org/linguistics/)
A searchable database of everything related to linguistics on the Net.

On-line Phonology Course
(http://www.stir.ac.uk/epd/higdox/stephen/phono/phonolg.htm)
A complete online phonology course (with sound too!) from Stirling University.

Speech on the Web
(http://fonsg3.let.uva.nl/Other_pages.html)
Numerous links related to phonetics and speech sciences.

Universal Survey of Languages
(http://www.teleport.com/~napoleon/)
A "general survey of the world's languages suitable for the linguistic beginner and expert alike."

Links

ESL Links Page for Students
(http://www.pacificnet.net/~sperling/student.html)

ESL Links Page for Teachers
(http://www.pacificnet.net/~sperling/links2.html)
Add your own favorite links to these interactive Web pages from the ESL Cafe.

ESL on the Internet
(http://www.artsci.wustl.edu/~langlab/ESL.old.html)
Splendid collection from Washington University in St. Louis.

ESLoop
(http://math.unr.edu/linguistics/esloop/esloop.html)
A collection of ESL/EFL Web sites, where each site is linked to the next.

Interesting Links for ESL Teachers
(http://polyglot.cal.msu.edu/mitesol/linkseslteachers.html)
Selection of links from Michigan Teachers of English to Speakers of Other Languages.

Kenji Kitao's Home Page
(http://148.88.14.7:80/staff/visitors/kenji/)
One of the very finest collection of links, from Doshisha University's Kenji Kitao.

Links to ESL/EFL/TESL/TEFL Links Pages (ITESLJ)
(http://www.aitech.ac.jp/~iteslj/Links/Links.html)
Astounding collection from the *Internet TESL Journal.*

Many ESL/EFL Links For Students
(http://www.aitech.ac.jp/~iteslj/ESL2.html)
Probably the best collection of ESL links in the world, brought to you by the *Internet TESL Journal.* Don't miss it!

Selected Links for ESL Students
(http://www.aitech.ac.jp/~iteslj/ESL.html)
Also from the *Internet TESL Journal,* this is the "best of the best."

Sites Neteachers Thought Were Cool
(http://math.unr.edu/linguistics/neteach.html)
A list of cool sites from the discussion group, Neteach-L.

Volterre Web Links for Learners
(http://www.wfi.fr/volterre/weblinklearners.html)
Hot collection of resources from Linda Thalman's Volterre-Fr. Highly recommended!

Volterre Web Links for Teachers
(http://www.wfi.fr/volterre/weblinktch.html)
More great links from Linda Thalman's Volterre-Fr. Don't miss it!

Webber Gate
(http://www.rede.com/eslgames/webgate.htm)
A good collection from Michael Bendel.

Yahoo's ESL Page
(http://www.yahoo.com/Education/Languages/English_as_a_Second_Language/)
Selection of ESL links from the one and only Yahoo.

Listening and Speaking

A Chance Meeting
(http://www.owlnet.rice.edu/~ling417/exercises/dialogue.html)
Watch a Quicktime clip and then answer the questions.

Integration of Reading, Listening, and Speaking Skills
(http://www.lang.uiuc.edu/r-li5/ESLproject/eslbeg.html)
Very innovative resource from Internet pioneer Rong-Chang Li.

Learning Oral English Online
(http://www.lang.uiuc.edu/r-li5/book/)
An online conversation book compiled for intermediate English language learners, from Rong-Chang Li.

TimeCast—The Real Audio Guide
(http://www.timecast.com/)
A complete listing of Real Audio broadcasts from all around the world. Highly recommended!

Literacy

The Center for Literacy
(http://www.libertynet.org/~literacy/Literacy.html)
Resources from Pennsylvania's oldest and the nation's largest community-based adult literacy organization.

The Literacy List
(http://www2.wgbh.org/mbcweis/LTC/ALRI/LiteracyList.html)
David J. Rosen's extensive review of literacy resources available on the Internet.

Literacy Publications
(http://www.sil.org/acpub/catalog/literacy.html)
Short bibliography from the Summer Institute of Linguistics.

National Institute for Literacy
(http://novel.nifl.gov/)
Comprehensive and searchable site from the National Institute for Literacy.

Literature

Aesop's Fables
(gopher://spinaltap.micro.umn.edu/11/Ebooks/By%20Title/aesop)
The full text of this classic in literature.

Children's Literature: Electronic Resources
(gopher://lib.nmsu.edu/11/.subjects/Education/.childlit)
Electronic versions of classics from such authors as Lewis Carroll, Joseph Conrad, Charles Dickens, and Arthur Conan Doyle.

Classics
(http://the-tech.mit.edu/Classics)
A searchable collection of almost 400 classical Greek and Roman texts.

Collected Works of Shakespeare
(http://www.gh.cs.usyd.edu.au/~matty/Shakespeare/)
A searchable full-text database of everything written by Mr. William Shakespeare. This site is a must!

English Literature Page
(http://humanitas.ucsb.edu/shuttle/english.html)
From Alan Liu of University of California, Santa Barbara; you'll find the full-text creations of works taught in English and American literature departments. Highly recommended!

Literature-Related Links
(http://www.cs.uidaho.edu/~connie/interests-lit.html)
Connie Hatley's comprehensive collection of links.

Tales of Wonder: Folk and Fairy Tales from Around the World
(http://www.ece.ucdavis.edu/~darsie/tales.html)
Entertaining archive of folk and fairy tales from many parts of the world.

Magazines

Discover Magazine
(http://www.enews.com:80/magazines/discover)
Online magazine of science.

Electronic Newsstand
(http://www.enews.com/)
Links to over 2,000 online magazines. This site is a must!

Entertainment Weekly Magazine
(http://www.pathfinder.com/@@70uJSHDS1QAAQHoY/ew)
Get the latest news from Hollywood.

National Geographic Online
(http://www.nationalgeographic.com/)
This online version of *National Geographic* is updated daily.

People Magazine
(http://www.pathfinder.com/@@q2Ms9aDP0wAAQHwY/people/)
Convenient source to find the latest info about Brad Pitt or Cindy Crawford!

Time Magazine
(http://www.pathfinder.com/@@wNe9a9B20QAAQHwY/time/)
Online version of *Time* magazine that includes back issues and daily news updates.

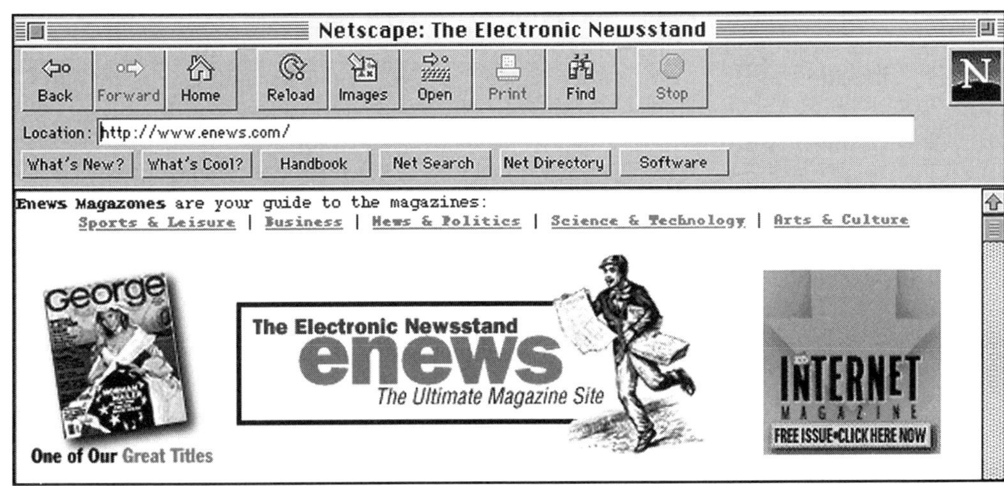

Meeting Other Teachers

ESL Email Connection for Teachers
(http://www.pacificnet.net/~sperling/guestbook.html)
Add your name to a growing list of ESL/EFL teachers from around the world.

ESL Teachers Home Pages
(http://www.aitech.ac.jp/~iteslj/Links/TeacherPages.html)
A database of ESL /EFL teacher's home pages from around the world.

Teacher Contact Database
(http://www.classroom.net/contact/)
A database where you can find other teachers who are interested in doing key pal exchanges, projects, and more.

Movies and Screenplays

Drew's Scripts-O-Rama
(http://home.cdsnet.net/~nikko11/nontable.htm)
The most comprehensive collection of screenplays found anywhere on the Net.

Scripts and Screenplays
(http://hollywoodu.com/script.htm)
Collection of scripts and screenplays from the Hollywood Film Institute.

Multicultural Issues

Diversity
(http://execpc.com/~dboals/diversit.html)
Dennis Boals's massive collection of multicultural resources. Highly recommended!

Hispanic Culture
(http://gpu.srv.ualberta.ca/~scoleman/culture.html)
Sheryl Coleman's page of Hispanic resources.

Multicultural Holidays: An Interactive Exhibit
(http://curry.edschool.Virginia.EDU/~insttech/ITpgm/projects/holidays/)
Includes Chinese New Year, Christmas, Hannukah, and Kwanzaa.

Multicultural Pavilion
(http://curry.edschool.virginia.edu:80/go/multicultural/home.html)
The University of Virginia's project to provide a resource for educators interested in multicultural issues. Highly recommended!

OneWorld Magazine
(http://www.envirolink.org/oneworld/index.html)
An online multicultural magazine that presents articles and images from around the world.

Saturn Hmong Page
(http://ww2.saturn.stpaul.k12.mn.us/hmong/sathmong.html)
Hmong dictionary, lesson plans, pictures, links and a student showcase make this site a special winner.

News and Newspapers

Asahi News
(http://www.asahi.com/english/english.html)
Get the latest news in English from one of Japan's leading papers.

The Bangkok Post
(http://www.bangkokpost.net/)
Live everyday from Bangkok, Thailand.

The Cambodian Times
(http://www.jaring.my/at-asia/camb_at_asia/camb_times/ct_list.html)
Online version of Cambodia's national newspaper.

China News Service
(http://www.chinanews.com/)
Great source for the latest news from Hong Kong and China.

CNN Interactive
(http://www.cnn.com)
One of the very best sources of news on the Net.

Compass Middle East Wire News Service
(http://www.compass-news.com/)
The latest news from the Middle East.

The Electronic Telegraph
(http://www.telegraph.co.uk/)
Top-notch paper from the UK. You need to register, but it's free.

The Hindu
(http://www.webpage.com/hindu/index.html)
Online edition of India's national newspaper.

ISN KidNews
(http://www.vsa.cape.com/~powens/KidNews.html)
News and current events for kids and teachers.

The Jerusalem Post
(http://www.jpost.co.il)
Online version of Israel's leading daily English newspaper.

Kyodo News
(http://www.kyodo.co.jp/)
Daily news from Tokyo, Japan.

Los Angeles Times
(http://www.latimes.com/HOME/)
Great online paper from my hometown, Los Angeles.

Nando Times
(http://www2.nando.net/nt/nando.cgi)
Another excellent daily online newspaper.

Newspapers on the Web
(http://www.intercom.com.au/intercom/newsprs/index.htm)
Comprehensive listing of newspapers from all over the world. Highly recommended.

The New York Times
(http://www.nytimes.com/)
Online version of New York's finest.

Panafrican News Agency
(http://www1.nando.net/ans/pana/index.html)
Up-to-date coverage of news from Africa.

Reuters
(http://www.reuters.com/)
News from one of the world's leading international news and financial information services company.

The Ultimate Collection of News Links
(http://pppp.net/links/news/)
Over 4,000 links to newspapers around the world, organized by continent and then by country and state/province.

USA Today
(http://www.usatoday.com)
Online edition of one of America's most popular daily newspapers.

Online Help

Ask an Expert
(http://www.askanexpert.com/p/ask.html)
Over 200 Web sites and e-mail addresses where students can find experts from the Amish to Zookeeping! Highly recommended!

Ask Cyberscout!
(http://www.mmhschool.com/teach/scoutf3.html)
From Macmillan/McGraw-Hill, Ask Cyberscout! is for K–8 teachers with current research assignments.

ESL Discussion Center
(http://www.eslcafe.com/discussion/)
Discussion and help for ESL/EFL teachers. Forums include Activities and Games, Computer-Assisted Language Learning, English for Specific Purposes, K–12, Learning/Teaching Material, and Teaching Tips. Very cool!

ESL Help Center
(http://www.pacificnet.net/~sperling/wwwboard2/wwwboard.html)
A place where students can quickly receive help from an international team of volunteer teachers from Australia, Austria, Canada, the Czech Republic, France, Hong Kong, Israel, Italy, Korea, Kuwait, Spain, and the U.S.A.

ESL Question Page
(http://www.pacificnet.net/~sperling/q.html)
My very own ESL question and answer page, maintained since December 1995.

Grammar Clinic
(http://www.lydbury.co.uk/grammar/contents.html_)
Edunet's grammar help page.

Grammar Hotline Directory
(http://www.infi.net/tcc/tcresourc/faculty/dreiss/writcntr/hotline.html)
Telephone numbers and e-mail addresses of teachers willing to answer short questions about writing.

Professor TOEFL's Fun Page
(http://www.slip.net/~caa/)
Each week, five questions are answered and posted to Professor TOEFL's Fun Page.

Writery by Email
(http://www.missouri.edu/~wleric/email.html)
Writing help via e-mail from a University of Missouri tutor.

Writime
(http://www.bgsu.edu/departments/writing-lab/writime.html)
Writing help from Bowling Green State University.

Poetry

BioPoem Exchange Project
(http://www.halcyon.com/ahcool/biopoem.html)
Poems created by students from all over the world. Highly recommended!

Combine Your Grammar and Poetry Skills
(http://home.sn.no/~andreasl/gram-po.htm)
Norway's Andrea Lund teaches students to write a 5-line poem.

English Poetry Database
(http://www.lib.virginia.edu/etext/epd/)
From the University of Virginia library, this is a full-text searchable database of hundreds of poems.

The Internet Poetry Archive
(http://sunsite.unc.edu/dykki/poetry/home.html)
Selection of poems from a number of contemporary poets.

Pizzaz!
(http://darkwing.uoregon.edu/~leslieob/pizzaz.html)
Great series of poetry links from Leslie Opp-Beckman.

Yahoo's Country and Cultures—Poetry
(http://www.yahoo.com/Arts/Humanities/Literature/Genres/Poetry/Countries_and_Cultures/)
Links to poetry from all over the world, brought to you by Yahoo.

Pronunciation

Alphabet
(http://www.edunet.com/english/grammar/alpha.html)
Anthony Hughes' pronunciation of the English alphabet, complete with sound files.

Dialect Accent Specialists
(http://plainfield.bypass.com/~dasinc/)
Information on the well-known accent reduction program developed by Dr. David Alan Stern.

Did the Cat Get Your Tongue?
(http://www.cuhk.hk/eltu/ELH/doc4.html)
Entertaining article on how to improve spoken English.

Pronunciation
(http://lc.ust.hk/~sac/lsdpron.htm)
Tips on the pronunciation of English.

Proverbs and Quotations

ESL Quote Page
(http://www.pacificnet.net/~sperling/cookie.pl.cgi)
ESL Cafe's collection of random quotes and proverbs from all over the world.

The Quotations Page
(http://www.starlingtech.com/quotes/)
One of the best collections on the Net, brought to you by Michael Moncur.

Russian Proverbs and Sayings
(http://solar.rtd.utk.edu/friends/literature/russian-proverbs.html)
Collection of Russian proverbs and sayings, from Russian author M. Dubrovin.

Some African Proverbs
(http://www.nd.edu/~ndasa/proverbs.html)
Selection of 18 African proverbs.

Public Speaking

Key Steps to an Effective Presentation
(http://access5.digex.net/~nuance/keystep1.html)
Informative article written by Stephen Eggleston.

Overcoming Speaking Anxiety in Meetings and Presentations
(http://www.all-biz.com/articles/anxiety.htm)
Lenny Laskowski's advice on how to combat anxiety.

The Speaker's Companion Reference Page
(http://www.lm.com/~chipp/spkrref.htm)
A useful list of reference sites valuable to anyone who speaks in public.

Ten Commandments of Presentations
(http://www.tagsys.com/Ads/strategic/tencommpres.html)
Ten useful tips from Strategic Communications.

Tips For Dealing With Nervousness
(http://www.indiana.edu/~ucstm/edminute/jparment1.html)
Excellent article by Julie Parmenter on how to overcome nervousness.

Your Body Speaks
(http://www.toastmasters.com/tm-body.htm)
Article on nonverbal communication from Tustin Toastmasters.

Publishers

Addison-Wesley
(http://www.aw.com/)

Athelstan Publications
(http://www.nol.net/~athel/athel.html)

Boswell
(http://www.boswell.com/index.html)

Cambridge University Press
(http://www.cup.cam.ac.uk/)

Cascadilla Press Linguistics Titles
(http://www.shore.net/~cascadil/linguistics.html)

Collins' Cobuild
(http://titania.cobuild.collins.co.uk/)

Columbia University Press
(http://www.columbia.edu/cu/cup/)

DynEd
(http://WWW.DYNED.COM)

Encomium Publications
(http://www.iac.net/~encomium/)

Everglory Publishing Company
(http://www.rede.com/eslgames/index.htm)

Exceller Software Corporation
(http://www.exceller.com/)

Exit Studio
(http://members.aol.com/ExitStudio/index.htm)

Gessler Publishing
(http://www.gessler.com/gessler/)

Heinle & Heinle
(http://www.thomson.com/heinle.html)

Holt, Rinehart & Winston College Language Publishers
(http://www.agoralang.com:2410/hrwcollege.html)

Houghton Mifflin Company
(http://www.hmco.com/)

Indiana University Press
(http://www.indiana.edu/~iupress/)

Longman
(http://www.aw.com/longman.html)

Macmillan
(http://www.mcp.com/)

McGraw-Hill
(http://www.mcgraw-hill.com/)

Merit Audio Visual
(http://www.meritav.com)

MIT Press: Linguistics
(http://www-mitpress.mit.edu/mitp/recent-books/linguistics/linguistics-toc.html)

OK! Software
(http://www.mdn.com/oksoftware/)

Opus Instruments
(http://www.gate.net/~opus/)

Oxford University Press English Language Teaching
(http://www1.oup.co.uk/cite/oup/elt/software/)

Prentice Hall Regents
(http://www.phregents.com/)

Princeton University Press
(http://pup.princeton.edu)

Pro Lingua Associates
(http://www.bookworld.com/proling.htm)

Romus Interactive
(http://ourworld.compuserve.com/homepages/Romus/)

Syracuse Language Systems
(http://www.syrlang.com/)

Thomson Publishing
(http://www.thomson.com/)

Transparent Language
(http://206.26.144.53/homepage.htm)

University of Chicago Press
(http://www.press.uchicago.edu)

University of Michigan Press
(http://www.press.umich.edu/)

World of Reading
(http://www.wor.com/)

Quizzes

CNN's News Quiz
(http://cnn.com/SEARCH/quiz/)
Daily quiz on the news from CNN. Highly recommended!

ESL Quiz Center
(http://www.pacificnet.net/~sperling/quiz)
Interactive quizzes on Current News, Geography, Grammar, History, Idioms, Slang, Words, People, Reading Comprehension, Science, Vocabulary, World Culture, and Writing. Don't miss it!

Fluency Through Fables
(http://www.comenius.com/fable/index.html)
Each month, you'll find a new fable and a variety of exercises to assist students.

On-Line Language Exercise
(http://www.ilcgroup.com/exercise.html)
Interactive English language exercises in Java from England's International House. Very cool!

Self-Study Quizzes for ESL Students
(http://www.aitech.ac.jp/~iteslj/quizzes/)
Great resource from the *Internet TESL Journal.*

Test Your English
(http://www.edunet.com/english/practice/test-ces.html)
A quiz from Edunet that contains 80 questions. Results are sent back by e-mail.

Resources

Adult Education ESL Teachers Guide
(http://humanities.byu.edu/elc/Teacher/TeacherGuideMain)
Lots of good information from Texas A&I University.

Dave's ESL Cafe
(http://www.eslcafe.com/)
Several interactive resources, including the ESL Graffiti Wall, ESL Question Page, ESL Idea Page, ESL Message Exchange, ESL Quiz Center, ESL Links Pages, ESL Help Center, ESL Email Connection Pages, ESL Discussion Center, and the ESL Job Center. Don't miss it!

English as a Second Language Home Page
(http://www.lang.uiuc.edu/r-li5/esl/)
Links, information, resources, and activities from the multitalented Rong-Chang Li of the University of Illinois at Urbana–Champaign.

English Language Teaching Resources
(http://www.tcom.ohiou.edu/OU_Language/teachers-language-engl.html)
Collection of resources from Ohio University.

ESL Virtual Catalog
(http://www.pvp.com/internet_resources.htm)
Directory of Internet ESL/EFL resources.

Foreign Language Teaching Resources
(http://babel.uoregon.edu/yamada/forlang.html)
Resources from Yamada Language Center at the University of Oregon.

Frizzy University Network (FUN)
(http://thecity.sfsu.edu/~funweb)
Excellent collection of resources for students and teachers, including tips on how to make a Web page and links to other resources. Students can even take FUN classes in writing and grammar. Don't miss it!

Kathy Schrock's Guide for Educators
(http://www.capecod.net/Wixon/wixon.htm)
Updated daily; you'll find a list of sites on the Internet useful for teachers.

Linguistic Funland TESL Page
(http://math.unr.edu/linguistics/tesl.html)
Extensive links (and more!) from Internet pioneer Kristina Pfaff-Harris. Highly recommended.

One World, One People
(http://members.aol.com/Jakajk/ESLLessons.html)
ESL/EFL teaching ideas, games, and resources.

Resources for English Language and Culture
(http://www.tcom.ohiou.edu/OU_Language/lang-english.html)
Super collection of resources from Ohio University's John McVicker.

Teachers Helping Teachers
(http://www.pacificnet.net/~mandel/)
Teaching tips and ideas for teachers. Don't forget to check out their IRC channel.

TESL/FL Resource Guide
(http://math.unr.edu/linguistics/mele.faq.html)
One of the very best collections of Frequently Asked Questions, from the newsgroup misc.education.language.english. Highly recommended!

Virtual English Center
(http://www.comenius.com/)
Brought to you by The Comenius Group; you'll find excellent resources such as the Weekly Idiom, Fluency Through Fables, and the E-mail Key Pal Connection.

VOLTERRE-FR
(http://www.wfi.fr/volterre)
Edited and published by Linda Thalman; you'll find some of the most extensive links and resources found anywhere on the Internet. Highly recommended!

School Directories

American College/University Admissions Office E-Mail Addresses
(http://www.beantown.com/AEGC/email/)
The most comprehensive available list of e-mail addresses of college and university admissions offices.

English Language Schools in Israel
(http://www.u-net.com/eflweb/israelad.htm)
American Center in Israel's list of Israeli English language schools.

HotList of K–12 Internet School Sites
(http://rrnet.com/~gleason/k12.html)
From Gleason Sackman, this is a listing of K–12 Web sites in the U.S.

Law Schools
(http://www.collegenet.com/geograph/law.html)
CollegeNet's collection of American law schools.

MBA Programs
(http://www.collegenet.com/new/geograph/mba.html)
Huge listing of American MBA programs, courtesy of CollegeNet.

Peterson's ESL Summer Programs 230 listings
(http://www.petersons.com/summerop/select/aca043se.html)
Listing of over 230 summer programs offering English as a second language classes. Highly recommended!

Study Abroad Directory
(http://www.studyabroad.com/)
Directory of programs from all over the world.

Study in the USA
(http://www.studyusa.com/tocstate.htm)
A listing of programs in all 50 states.

U.S. Two-Year Colleges
(http://www.sp.utoledo.edu/twoyrcol.html)
The most comprehensive listing of American 2-year colleges, with nearly 600 listings.

World-Wide English Language Schools
(http://www.u-net.com/eflweb/tefl21.htm)
A global directory of schools teaching English to non-native speakers.

Schools—Individual ESL Programs

American Academy of English
(http://www.americad.com/)

Arizona State University
(http://www.asu.edu/xed/alcp/esl.html)

Arkansas State University
(http://math.unr.edu/linguistics/astate-cesl.html)

Auckland English Academy, New Zealand
(http://www.english.co.nz/)

Austin English Academy
(http://members.aol.com/austinea/index.htm)

Boston Language Institute
(http://www.boslang.com/)

Bournemouth International Language College
(http://www.bucc.co.uk/vbp/bilc/index.html)

Brigham Young University
(http://humanities.byu.edu/elc/cyberCenter)

The British Council
(http://www.britcoun.org/english/index.htm)

Cairns College of English, Australia
(http://www.cairns.aust.com/cce/index.html)

California State University, Hayward
(http://www.alp.csuhayward.edu/)

California State University, San Marcos
(http://coyote.csusm.edu/Extended_Studies/alciweb/)

California State University, Northridge
(http://www.csun.edu/~hfoao006/)

City University of Hong Kong Language Institute
(http://www.CityU.edu.hk/li/oldindex.htm)

Clarkson University, New York
(http://www.clarkson.edu/~english/)

Colorado State University
(http://yuma.acns.colostate.edu/~cwis85/IEP.html)

Columbia College, Vancouver, Canada
(http://web20.mindlink.net/ccelc/)

Curry College
(http://www.curry.edu:8080/pal/pal.html)

De La Salle Language Institute, Minnesota
(http://140.190.131.87/)

Dublin Language Centre, Ireland
(http://www.dlc.ie/)

ECC Thailand
(http://www.eccthai.com)

ELS Language Centers
(http://www.els.com/)

English Country School
(http://ourworld.compuserve.com/homepages/ecs/)

English Learning Experience in Nova Scotia
(http://www.grassroots.ns.ca/~adnet/edu/elens/welcome.html)

Fields College
(http://www.fieldscollege.com/~esl/)

Fort Richmond Collegiate, Canada
(http://home.cc.umanitoba.ca/~umturne5/)

Francis Marion University, South Carolina
(http://www.fmarion.edu/academic/other/IEI.htm)

GL:OBE School of Languages
(http://www.lookup.com/Homepages/82009/home.html)

Gonzaga University, Spokane, Washington
(http://www.gonzaga.edu/office/isp/elc/)

Harbourside College, Vancouver
(http://www.harbourside.com/)

Harvest Park International College, Canada
(http://207.34.144.2/harvest/)

Hawai'i Community College
(http://www.hawcc.hawaii.edu/hawcc/IEPinfo.html)

Hunter College
(http://www.hunter.cuny.edu/ieli/)

Indiana University
(http://www.indiana.edu/~celtiep/iep.html)

INTERLINK Language Center
(http://www.guilford.edu/internationalstudents/INTERLINK.html)

International House
(http://www.ilcgroup.com/)

Iowa State University
(http://www.public.iastate.edu/~tesling/ieop.html)

Johns Hopkins University
(http://jhunix.hcf.jhu.edu/~dshiffma/esl.html)

Johnson County Community College, Kansas
(http://www.johnco.cc.ks.us/docs/English.html)

King's English Language Schools
(http://www.kings-group.co.uk/)

Lincoln University, San Francisco
(http://www.lincolnuca.edu/)

Manchester College of Arts and Technology
(http://www.u-net.com/eflweb/norwest.htm)

Maple Leaf Academy, Canada
(http://www.syz.com/mla/)

Marshall University
(http://www.marshall.edu/esli/)

Marycrest International University
(http://www.mcrest.edu/~alcdept/alcpage.html)

Maryland English Institute
(http://www.inform.umd.edu:8080/EdRes/Colleges/ARHU/Depts/MEI)

Meads School of English, England
(http://www.mistral.co.uk/meads/)

Memorial University of Newfoundland
(http://www.mun.ca/elss/)

Michigan State University
(http://polyglot.cal.msu.edu/ELC/)

MiraCosta College
(http://www.miracosta.cc.ca.us/home/krippberger/ESLResources.html)

Monterey Institute of International Studies
(http://www.miis.edu/)

Muskingum College
(http://www.muskingum.edu/~cal/davep.html)

Northeastern Illinois University
(http://www.ecnet.net/users/uwwwelp/)

Northern State University, South Dakota
(http://www.northern.edu/esl/esl.html)

North Park College, Chicago
(http://www.npcts.edu/acad/esl/)

The Ohio Program of Intensive English (OPIE)
(http://www.tcom.ohiou.edu/OU_Language/050PIE.html)

Old Dominion University
(http://www.odu.edu/gnusers/teevan/elchtml.htm)

Oregon State University
(http://www.orst.edu/Dept/eli/)

Oxford University Language Centre
(http://info.ox.ac.uk/departments/langcentre/)

Penobscot School, Rockland, Maine
(http://www.midcoast.com/~penobsct/)

Queen Margaret College
(http://www.qmced.ac.uk/inter/www/english_intro.htm)

Rice University
(http://www.rice.edu/esl/)

Salisbury School of English
(http://www.u-net.com/eflweb/salisad.htm)

San Diego State University
(http://mail.sdsu.edu/~ali/index.html)

Seattle Central Community College
(http://www.sccd.ctc.edu/~ccglobal/)

Southwest Texas State University
(http://www.ideal.swt.edu/esl/eng_sec_lang.html)

Tellus Language College, Vancouver, Canada
(http://www.telluslc.com/)

University at Buffalo
(http://wings.buffalo.edu/gse/eli/)

University at North Carolina, Charlotte
(http://www.coe.uncc.edu/~brmattin/elti.html)

University of Arizona
(http://wacky.ccit.arizona.edu/~cesl/capestat.html)

University of Arkansas at Little Rock
(http://www.ualr.edu/~ielp/index.html)

University of California, Berkeley
(http://violet.berkeley.edu/~cwp/summer.html)

University of California, Irvine
(http://www.unex.uci.edu/~unex/esl/)

University of California, Riverside
(http://www.unex.ucr.edu/iephomepage.html)

University of Dayton
(http://www.udayton.edu/~cip/index.htm)

University of Delaware
(http://www.udel.edu/IntlProg/eli/1elipage.html)

University of Hawai'i
(http://www.lll.hawaii.edu/esl/)

University of Houston
(http://bentley.uh.edu/English/LCC/home.htm)

University of Illinois, Champaign–Urbana
(http://deil.lang.uiuc.edu/iei/)

University of Limerick, Ireland
(http://www.ul.ie/~clc/)

University of Maine
(http://www.ume.maine.edu/~iei)

University of Montana
(http://www.umt.edu/nss/viewbook/eli.htm)

University of North Carolina
(http:www.coe.uncc.edu/~tcbriggs/elti.html)

University of Northern Iowa
(http://iscssun.uni.edu/ciep/)

University of Pennsylvania
(http://www.sas.upenn.edu/elp/)

University of South Florida
(http://quijote.lang.usf.edu/~elimain/index.html)

University of Surrey
(http://www.surrey.ac.uk/ELI/eli.html)

University of Tennessee at Chattanooga
(http://www.utc.edu/esldept/esl2.html)

University of Texas, Arlington
(http://elilab.uta.edu/)

University of Utah
(http://www.dce.utah.edu/text/eli/)

University of Washington, Seattle
(http://weber.u.washington.edu/~esl/)

Vancouver English Centre
(http://www.worldtel.com/vec/home.html)

Vancouver Language Institute
(http://www.imag.net/~vli/)

Victoria University of Wellington, New Zealand
(http://www.vuw.ac.nz/eli/)

Washington State University
(http://www.wsu.edu:8080/~ialc/)

Wayne State University
(http://www.eli.wayne.edu/)

Winfield College, Vancouver, Canada
(http://www.WinfieldCollege.com/)

World Learning, Vermont
(http://www.worldlearning.org)

Songs and Music

Digital Tradition Folk Song Database
(http://www.deltablues.com/dbsearch.html)
A searchable database of over 5,622 songs.

Disney Song Lyrics
(http://zeus.informatik.uni-frankfurt.de/%7Efp/Disney/Lyrics/)
Lyrics from many of Disney's classic animated films.

Grendel's Lyric Archive
(http://homepage.seas.upenn.edu/~avernon/lyrics.html)
Huge collection of song lyrics.

Student Internet Projects

Amy Ogasawara's ESL Students' Projects
(http://www.miyazaki-mic.ac.jp/~aogasawa/projects.html)
Research project from students in Japan.

Applied Information Science Student Projects
(http://www.miyazaki-mic.ac.jp/faculty/kisbell/classes/electronicguide.html)
Student-created guidebook on Miyazaki, Japan, with info on restaurants, department stores, local foods, museums, and surfing.

Book Reviews by ESL Students
(http://www.aec.ukans.edu/staff/cheacock/real_rdg/real_rdg.html)
Book reviews by adult, English-as-a-second-language learners at the University of Kansas.

The Cutting Edge: Multimedia
(http://www.chorus.cycor.ca/Duber/students/classpage.html)
HTML creations from Jim Duber's summer ESL class at UC Berkeley.

Dave's ESL Writing Class
(http://www.csun.edu/~hcesl004/CSUN.html)
Pictures and biographies from one of my own ESL writing classes at California State University, Northridge.

English Foundation Programme
(http://www.cityu.edu.hk/li/topics/topics.htm)
Argumentative essays written by students taking the English Foundation Programme in Hong Kong.

Famous Personages in Japan
(http://www.kyoto-su.ac.jp/information/famous)
Very innovative project from Thomas Robb's students at Kyoto Sangyo University.

Robagoya Kids
(http://www.iijnet.or.jp/robagoya/kidspage.htm)
Student writings and photos from Robagoya English school in Japan.

Sanno/OU students
(http://www.tcom.ohiou.edu/OU_Language/project.sanno.html)
Written messages of introduction from students of Sanno College in Japan.

Student Projects
(http://prwww.ncook.k12.il.us/ESL/projects.html)
These projects from the ESL students at Pleasant Ridge School include Columbus Trivia, Halloween, Poetry, and Author Study.

Student Stories
(http://www.scoe.otan.dni.us/cdlp/visalia/studcont.htm)
Edited and unedited student stories from Visalia Adult School.

Writing for the World
(http://icarus.uic.edu/~kdorwick/world.html)
Excellent source from University of Chicago's Keith Dorwick.

Teacher Training

Adult Education ESL Teachers Guide
(http://humanities.byu.edu/elc/Teacher's/Teacher'sGuideMain)
Informative guide, especially for the novice ESL/EFL teacher, written by C. Ray Graham and Mark M. Walsh.

Best Teacher Description
(http://humanities.byu.edu/elc/Teacher/BestTeacher)
A list of characteristics and techniques that make a successful teacher.

Canadian Cooperative for Language and Cultural Studies, Toronto
(http://ourworld.compuserve.com:80/homepages/CCLCS/)
TESL training in Toronto, Canada.

Centre for English Language Studies, University of Manchester
(http://www.man.ac.uk/CELSE/)
TESL/TEFL training in the U.K.

Centres for UCLES Language Teaching Awards
(http://www.edunet.com/ciltsrsa/centres.html)
Very comprehensive listing of world-wide training centers for the University of Cambridge examinations. Includes Asia, Australasia, Middle East, North Africa, South Africa, Turkey, and the Americas (North, South, and Central).

Distance Learning Programs
(http://www.wfi.fr/volterre/distancelearning.html)
VOLTERRE-FR's listing of distance learning programs in TESL.

ELC Distance Learning Courses in TEFL/TESL & EFL
(http://www.addnet.demon.co.uk/elc/)
TEFL Certificate and Diploma courses available by distance learning.

International House TEFL Training Courses
(http://www.ilcgroup.com/ILC_Teachers1.html)
TEFL training courses all over the world, including the RSA/Cambridge Certificate, Diploma, and TEFL Methodology courses.

New World Teachers
(http://www.goteach.com)
TEFL training school located in San Francisco.

Pilgrims
(http://www.pilgrims.co.uk/)
Teacher training in the U.K.

School for International Training
(http://www.pilgrims.co.uk)
A variety of training programs in Brattleboro, Vermont.

Teacher Training for TEFL (in France)
(http://www.wfi.fr/volterre/teachtrain.html)
Listing of TESL certificate programs in France.

TEFL Training Course by ELS
(http://www.els.com/intltefl.htm)
TEFL certificate program from "one of America's leading intensive English programs."

Training to Teach English as a Second Language
(http://144.96.225.66/esltrain.html)
Listing (including the prices) of some of the ESL certificate programs.

University of Birmingham
(http://www.bham.ac.uk/CELS/TESFL_OLP.htm)
Distance program leading to the M.A. in TES/FL, with courses offered in Japan, Korea, and Taiwan, and soon, Thailand.

University of Cambridge Awards
(http://www.edunet.com/ciltsrsa/awards.html)
Information on the Certificate in Teaching English as a Foreign Language to Adults, Certificate for Overseas Teachers of English, Diploma for Overseas Teachers of English, and Diploma in Teaching English as a Foreign Language.

Testing and Assessment

Assessment and Evaluation on the Internet
(http://www.cua.edu/www/eric_ae/intbod.htm)
Very comprehensive assortment of links in various categories, including language assessment.

The Evaluation Assistance Center East
(http://www.gwu.edu/~eaceast/)
Assistance to educators working with English Language Learners (ELLs) in grades K–12.

Language Testing
(http://www.ling.lancs.ac.uk/staff/visitors/kenji/test.htm)
Another useful resource from Kenji and Kathleen Kitao.

The Language Tester's Guide to Cyberspace
(http://www.surrey.ac.uk/ELI/cybertxt.html)
Review of testing sites on the Web from the University of Surrey. Highly recommended!

Language Tests
(http://www.cal.org/CAL/HTML/RESEARCH/tests.htm)
From the Center for Applied Linguistics; links include the Basic English Skills Test (BEST) and the Foreign Language Test Development (Speaking Tests).

Language Tests for English Language Learners
(http://www.tcom.ohiou.edu/OU_Language/englishTests.html)
More help from Ohio University's John McVicker.

Resources in Language Testing
(http://www.surrey.ac.uk/ELI/ltr.html)
Excellent collection and review of language testing sites on the Web. Not to be missed!

Theatre and Drama

Plays Online
(http://www.brookes.ac.uk/VL/theatre/index.htm)
Complete texts in English, French, German, Greek, Italian, and Spanish.

Yahoo's Plays
http://www.yahoo.com/Arts/Drama/Plays/
Yahoo's collection of links to online plays.

TOEFL

Kaplan's TOEFL Page
(http://www.kaplan.com/intl/toefl_top.html)
Information on the TOEFL test from one of the world's leading prep companies.

Kaplan's Top 10 TOEFL Tips
(http://www.kaplan.com/intl/toefl_top_ten.html)
TOEFL advice from Kaplan Educational Centers.

TOEFL Online
(http://www.toefl.org/)
The official TOEFL Web site from Educational Testing Service. Includes test dates and practice questions.

TOEFL Prep Page
(http://www.okanagan.bc.ca/ce-inter/esl/toefl/toefl_prep.html)
Online TOEFL practice for users with Shockwave.

TOEIC
(http://www.toeic-usa.com)
TOEIC info from International Communications, Inc.

Tongue Twisters

English Tongue-Twisters
(http://www.wu-wien.ac.at/usr/h93/h9325997/fun/twisters.html)
Small collection from the Technical University in Vienna, Austria.

International Collection of Tongue Twisters
(http://www.uibk.ac.at/c/c7/c704/qo/people/_mr/twister/index.html)
Michael Reck's collection includes tongue twisters in Bulgarian, Croatian, Czech, Dutch, English, Finnish, French, German, Hungarian, Irish, Italian, Japanese, Polish, Portuguese, Russian, Serbian, Spanish, and Swedish.

PIZZAZ! Tongue Twisters
(http://darkwing.uoregon.edu/~leslieob/twisters.html)
Tongue twister activity from Leslie Opp-Beckman.

Tongue Twister Database
(http://www.geocities.com/Athens/8136/tonguetwisters.html)
Collection of over 100 tongue twisters.

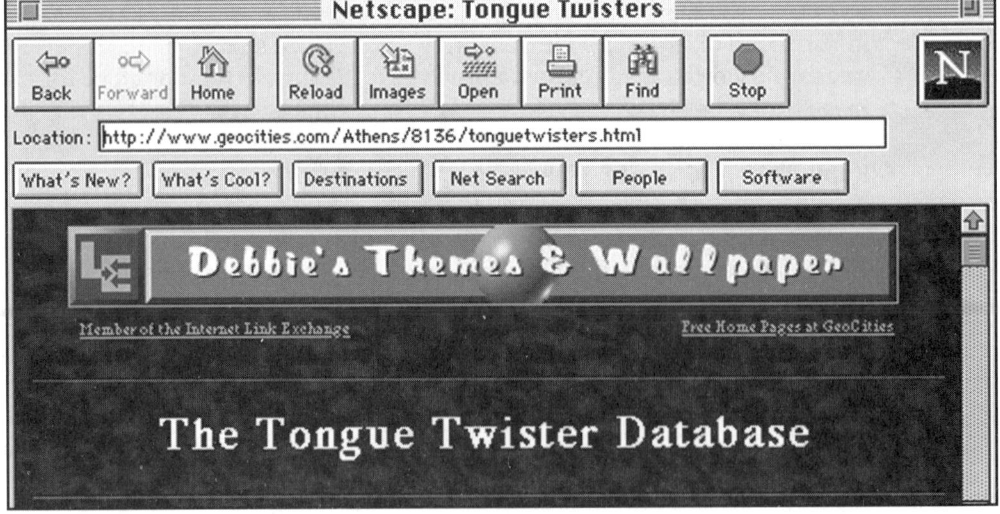

U.S. Immigration

Immigration Information
(http://www2.wgbh.org/mbcweis/immigrants.html)
Great links from the community-wide Education and Information Service.

United States Citizenship
(http://www.state.mn.us/ebranch/ssac/english/citizen.html)
Information on how to become a U.S. citizen.

U.S. Immigration and Naturalization Service
(http://www.usdoj.gov/ins/index.html)
The official home page of the U.S. Immigration and Naturalization Service. Don't miss their section of Frequently Asked Questions.

Video

Desktop Video Conferencing
(http://www.coe.missouri.edu/~cjw/video/index.htm)
From the College of Education at University of Missouri–Columbia, this guide teaches you everything you need to know on desktop video conferencing.

Ideas on Using Videos
(http://www.aitech.ac.jp/~iteslj/Lessons/Tatsuki-Video.html)
Donna Tatsuki's article published in the *Internet TESL Journal.*

Techniques for Teaching with Video
(http://www.phregents.com/techniqu.html)
Five techniques—Freeze Frame, Sound Only, Silent Viewing, Jigsaw Viewing, and Normal Viewing—from Prentice Hall Regents.

Using Video with English Language Learners
(http://www.kqed.org/fromKQED/Cell/Learning/english.html)
Tips on how to use video in the classroom.

Why Video in the Classroom?
(http://www.phregents.com/tguide.html)
More excellent help from Prentice Hall Regents.

Vocabulary, Idioms, and Slang

About Terms
(http://www.youngie.com/terms.htm)
List of British slang and expressions.

American Slanguages
(http://www.slanguage.com/)
Local slang from cities across the United States, as well as Australia, Canada, England, Ireland, and South Africa. Highly recommended!

Animal Idioms
(http://www.edunet.com/english/ practice/rside/V_animaq.html)
Online exercise to help students learn expressions containing animal terminology.

Cobuild Idiom of the Day
(http://titania.cobuild.collins.co.uk/Idiom.html)
New idiom each day from the newly published *Cobuild Dictionary of Idioms.*

College Slang
(gopher://wiretap.Spies.COM/00/Library/Article/Language/slang.col)
Collection of about 130 popular words used by American college students.

Cool Word of the Day
(http://www.edu.yorku.ca/~wotd)
A cool, new vocabulary word is taught each day. You can also view past words.

The Daily Dose Vocabulary Builder
(http://www.mrshowbiz.com/dailydose/vbdictionary/vocab.html)
Another useful site for learning a new word each day. You can also search their archives.

ESL Cafe's Random Idiom Page
(http://www.pacificnet.net/~sperling/idioms.cgi)
Hundreds of idioms are available at the click of a mouse, brought to you by Dennis Oliver of the American Language and Culture Program at Arizona State University.

Focusing on Words
(http://www.wordfocus.com/)
John G. Robertson's unique site helps students experience the wonder of words by focusing on the Latin and Greek elements used in English.

Idiom Bank
(http://deil.lang.uiuc.edu/exchange/contributions/learning/reference/index.html)
Another superb collection of idioms from Dennis Oliver.

Kiwi Words
(http://www.cs.caltech.edu/~john-t/just_for_fun/kiwi_words.html)
A comprehensive listing of New Zealand English, brought to you by John Thornley.

Merriam-Webster's Word of the Day
(http://www-lj.eb.com/cgi-bin/mwwod.pl)
Daily word includes pronunciation, example usage, and interesting information. Highly recommended!

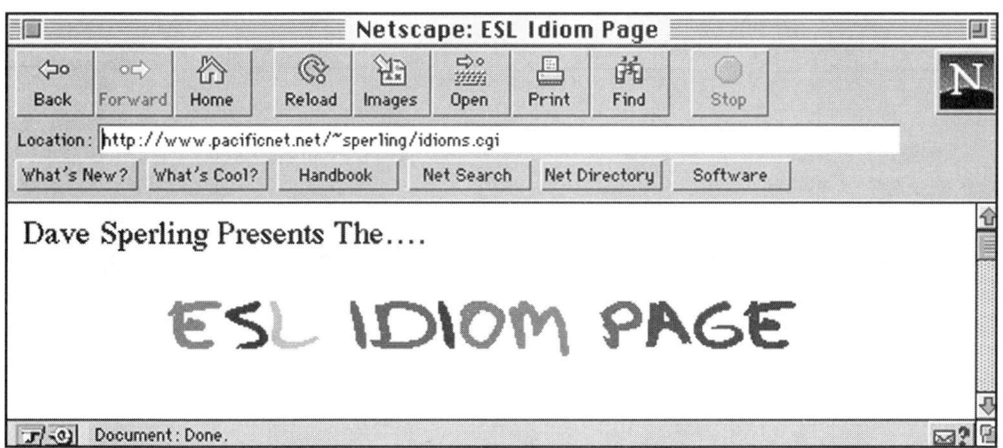

Popspeak
(http://www.blender.com/blender1.1/digest/popspeak/popspeak1.html)
Excellent site to learn the use of pop-cultural references.

Street Speak
(http://www.jayi.com/jayi/Fishnet/StreetSpeak/)
A terrific site for keeping up with the latest slang. Submissions, by the way, are welcome.

Surfing Slang
(http://www.malibu-rum.com/dude.htm)
Some lessons on the language of surfing slang. Cowabunga dude!

Truck Driving Slang
(http://www.ai.sri.com/~lau/trucks/slang.shtml)
A place to find out the meaning of a "4-wheeler with the greasy side up in the hammer lane."

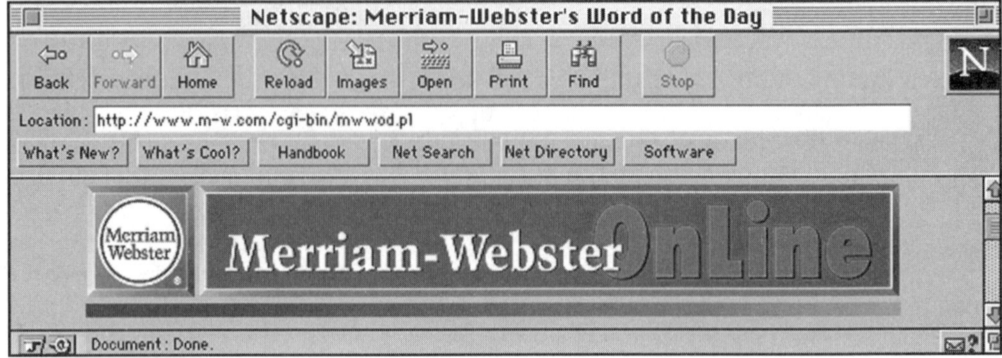

The Weekly Idiom
(http://www.comenius.com/idiom/index.html)
Each week The Comenius Group teaches a new idiom that includes an audio file for Windows and Macintosh.

Writing

DeVry's Online Writing Support Center
(http://www.devry-phx.edu/lrnresrc/dowsc/)
A page devoted to helping people understand how the Internet can enrich their writing.

Electric Postcard
(http://postcards.www.media.mit.edu/Postcards/Welcome.html)
Students can practice writing by sending virtual postcards to their friends and teachers. Lots of fun!

ESL Graffiti Wall
(http://www.pacificnet.net/~sperling/wall.html)
Students and teachers can add "graffiti" to a virtual wall.

Five Tools for Writing Timed Essays
(http://splavc.spjc.cc.fl.us/hooks/hooksessay.html)
Jeff Hook's tips on writing an academic essay.

On-Line Resources for Writers
(http://webster.commnet.edu/writing/writing.htm)
A list of online resources recommended by the English faculty of Capital Community-Technical College in Hartford.

Pizzaz!
(http://darkwing.uoregon.edu/~leslieob/pizzaz.html)
Pizzaz!, created by Leslie Opp-Beckman, is "dedicated to providing creative writing activities and copyable (yes, copyable!) handouts for use in the classroom." Highly recommended!

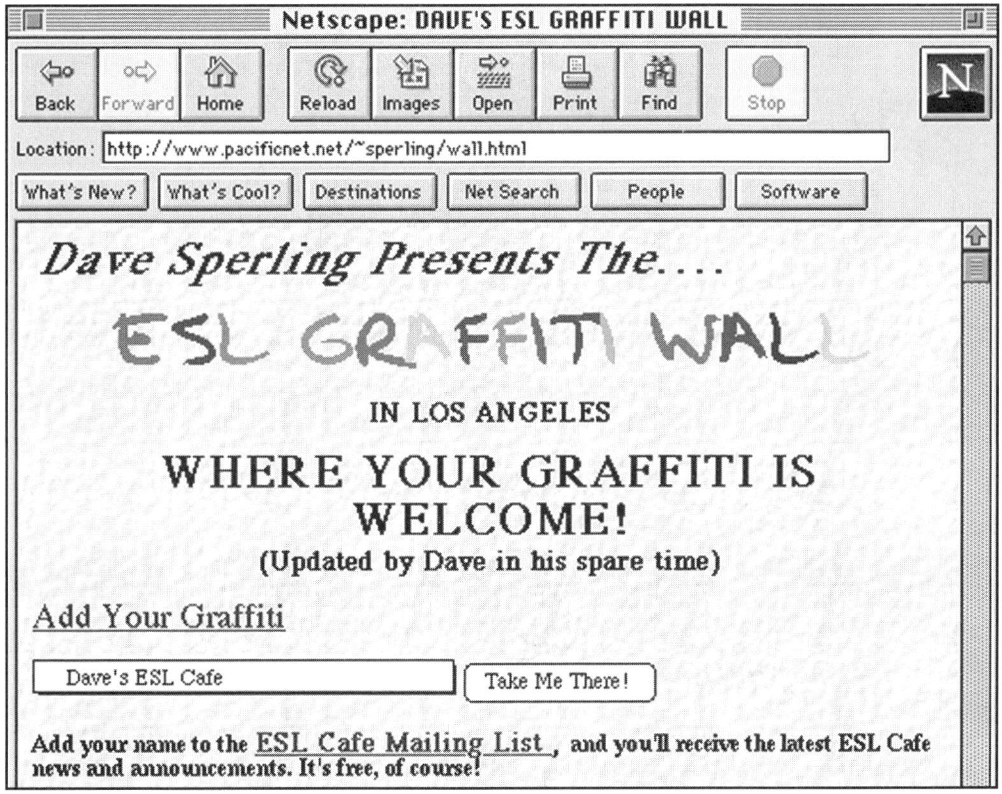

Punctuation
(http://sti.larc.nasa.gov/html/Chapt3/Chapt3-TOC.html)
Great place to learn about commas, colons, and dashes.

Purdue University On-line Writing Lab
(http://owl.trc.purdue.edu/by-topic.html)
Brought to you by the Purdue University Writing Lab, this is probably one of the very best writing resources available on the Web. Highly recommended!

Sample Letters
(http://www.coe.uncc.edu/~brmattin/adds.html)
Sample letters in English from the English Training Institute at UNC Charlotte.

Sample Student Papers
(http://www.ecnet.net/users/uwwwelp/practice.htm)
Student journals and the first and second drafts of student papers from the English Language program at Northeastern Illinois University.

Webster's Online Spell Checker
(http://www.goldendome.net/Tools/WebSter/)
Check your spelling online!

Writer's Guide on the Essay
(http://webserver.maclab.comp.uvic.ca/writersguide/Essay/EssaysTOC.html)
Essay writing guide from The Department of English, University of Victoria.

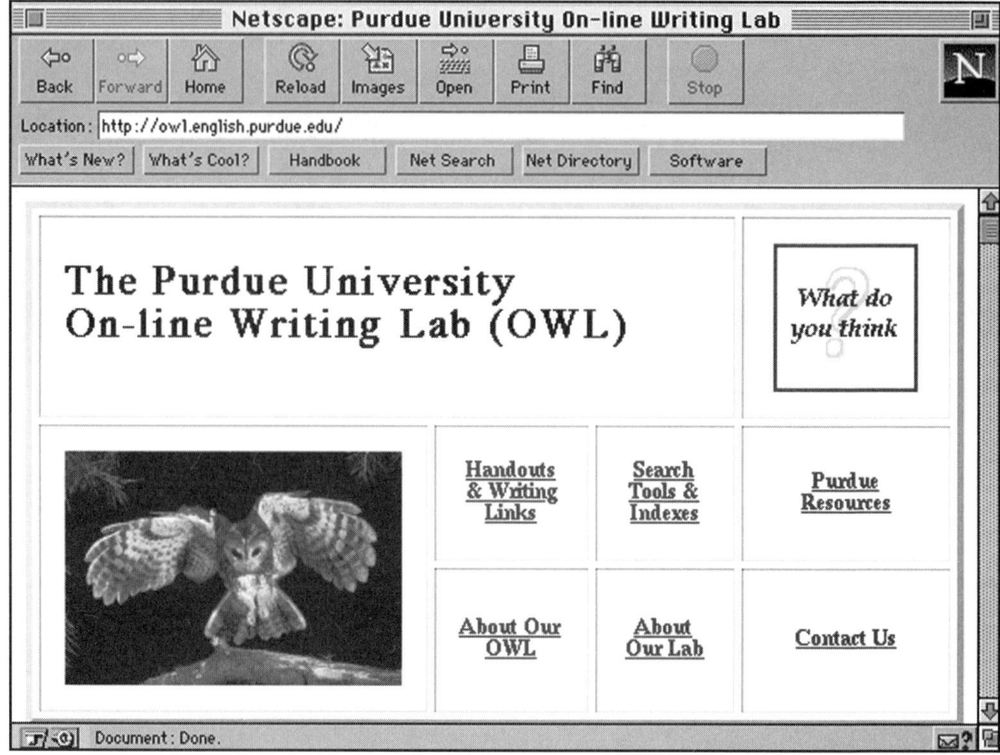

Writer's Web
(http://www.urich.edu/~writing/wweb.html)
A must for anyone who writes. Sections include Generating Ideas, Drafting and Organizing Papers, Focusing and Connecting Ideas, Creating and Supporting an Argument, Editing a Draft, Punctuation, Sentence Structure and Mechanics, Editing for Clarity and Style, Documentation, and Using Sources Effectively. Highly recommended!

Writing Help
(http://www.hut.fi/~rvilmi/LangHelp/Writing/)
And another excellent resource from Ruth Vilmi.

Writing Resources on the Web
(http://www.indiana.edu/~celtiep/resources.html)
Some really good writing links for ESL students.

Jobs on the Net

> *"I've actually gotten a number of unsolicited ESL/EFL/ESOL-related job offers from the Internet and I've accepted a few of them. I'm not raking in the dough or anything like that, but it is still nice."*
>
> Meg Gam
> American Language Institute, New York
> teacher@amanda.dorsai.org

Looking for a teaching job? You'll find the Web one of the best resources for up-to-date job announcements, as well as the latest information on where to teach. You can even keep your resume online for the viewing pleasure of potential employers. Here is a list of some resources that will help you get started on your job hunt.

Categories

Africa
Asia
Canada
China
Czech Republic
Europe
General—ESL/Education Related
Hong Kong
Indonesia
Information
Japan
Job Interview
K–12 Overseas
Korea
Latin America
Middle East
Miscellaneous
Resume
Singapore
Taiwan
Thailand
Volunteer

Africa

Africa Online Jobs
(http://www.africaonline.com/AfricaOnline/jobs.html)
African job listings in a variety of fields, including education.

Employment in Africa
(http://www.sas.upenn.edu/African_Studies/Travel/Employment_9976.html)
A page of employment opportunities in Africa.

International Volunteer Opportunities
(http://k12s.phast.umass.edu/~masag/1504o.html)
Volunteer opportunities from World Teach in various regions of the world, including Africa.

Asia

Asian Career Web Forum
(http://www.rici.com/acw/)
Presented by International Career Information, Inc.; you'll find opportunities in almost every region of Asia.

Asia-Net
(http://www.asia-net.com/jobs.html)
Positions for individuals fluent in Japanese, Chinese, and Korean.

EFL in Asia
(http://www.soback.kornet.nm.kr/~wiegand/9ef/asia.htm)
Hall Houston's excellent resource of links and information about teaching in Asia.

English Language Teaching in Asia
(gopher://gopher.nectec.or.th:70/11/lists)
Archive from the mailing list, ELTASIA-L: English Language Teaching in Asia.

English Teaching Programs in the Far East
(http://www.umich.edu/~icenter/tefl94ic.htm#FarEast)
Handout by William Nolting and Jeannine Lorenger from the University of Michigan's International Center.

Private Language Schools in East Asia
(http://www.umich.edu/~icenter/tefl94ic.htm#PrivateEastAsia)
More info from the University of Michigan's International Center.

Teaching English in Asia Pacific
(http://asiafacts.kingston.net/)
Help in finding a teaching position in Japan, Korea, Taiwan, Singapore, or Hong Kong, from Robert Burton, President of Asia Facts Unlimited.

Canada

ESL Opportunities in Canada
(www.tesl.ca/jobs.htm)

China

Career China
(http://www.globalvillager.com/villager/CC.html)
Job openings in China, Taiwan, Hong Kong, and beyond.

Chinajob
(http://www.north.net/chinajob/)
This nonprofit organization is run by China's State Bureau of Foreign Experts and serves as an employment agency for foreigners who want to work in China.

China-Net Positions
(http://www.asia-net.com/china-net.html)
Especially useful for those fluent in Chinese.

Czech Republic

Czech Republic
(http://www.jobs.cz/english_welcome.html)
Help from the very first job server in the Czech Republic.

Europe

The Central European Teaching Program
(http://www.beloit.edu/~cetp)
A nonprofit, volunteer organization that has been working to provide English teachers to Hungary and Romania.

Foreign Languages Teacher Training College, Poland
(http://cksr.ac.bialystok.pl/flattic/)
Database for ESL/EFL teachers in the Central Eastern European region.

Lancon English Language Consultancy
(http://alf.tel.hr/lancon/)
Information about teaching English in Croatia.

The Language Job Market
(http://www.vol.it/linguanet/jobs/job.htm)
Teaching positions in Italy.

Positions Mainly in Eastern Europe, Russia, and the NIS
(http://www.umich.edu/~icenter/tefl94ic.htm#EasternEurope)
More useful info from the University of Michigan's International Center.

Teach ESL in Central Europe
(http://144.96.225.66/eslceneur.html)

Teaching in Finland
(http://www.u-net.com/eflweb/finland0.htm)
Information on teaching in Finland, published by EFLWEB.

Teaching in Hungary
(http://www.u-net.com/eflweb/hungary.htm)
Another good article from EFLWEB.

Teaching in Italy
(http://www.mclink.it/com/reporter/index.html)
Information on teaching in Italy, from Reporter Publishing.

Teaching in Poland
(http://www.americad.com/)
Information about teaching in Poland, from the Academy of English.

Teaching in Spain
(http://www.u-net.com/eflweb/spain0.htm)
Sara Lowe's helpful advice on how to find a teaching job in Spain.

Teaching in Turkey
(http://www.bilkent.edu.tr/prv/bilkent-cwis/elea/jobs.html)

General (ESL/Education Related)

The Academic Employment Network
(http://www.academploy.com/)
You can search for teaching positions in the U.S., as well as add a free position announcement.

Agora Language Marketplace Employment Page
(http://www.agoralang.com:2410/agora/employment.html)
Language-related employment listings, including ESL/EFL.

BEN Employment Opportunities
(http://tism.bevc.blacksburg.va.us/employment.html)
Employment links and information from the Bilingual ESL Network.

California State University Employment Board
(http://csueb.sfsu.edu/csueb.html)
List of job openings at the campuses of California State University.

The Chronicle of Higher Education
(http://chronicle.merit.edu/.ads/.links.html)
Job openings from the highly respected Chronicle of Higher Education.

Education Jobs
(http://www.camrev.com.au/share/edu.html)
Educational job listings from Australia's International Academic Job Market.

EduNet's Education Employment in California
(http://ccnet4.ccnet.com/~pstrader/)
K–12 positions in California.

EF Employment Opportunities
(http://www.ef.com/jobs/jobs_com.html)
Job opportunities from the world's largest private English school.

ELS Job Opportunities
(http://www.els.com/intlempl.htm)
Listing of current positions available throughout the world with ESL Language Centers.

ESL Job Center
(http://www.pacificnet.net/~sperling/jobcenter.html)
Job announcements, information, links, discussion, and more.

ESL Jobs: Offered
(http://www.pacificnet.net/~sperling/wwwboard4/wwwboard.html)
Teaching positions from all around the world. Updated daily.

ELT Job Vacancies
(http://www.edunet.com/jobs/)
Edunet International's excellent listing of ESL/EFL positions.

Employment Opportunities for Language Teachers
(http://www.csun.edu/~hcedu013/employment.html)
Martin Levine's collection of links to ESL/EFL job opportunities.

Employment Resources for Language Teachers
(http://www.tcom.ohiou.edu/OU_Language/teachers-job.html)
Links from Ohio University.

Eric's International Teaching Opportunities
(http://www.ericsp.org/international.html)
Good information from Eric Clearinghouse on teaching and teacher education.

ESL Jobs
(gopher://rodent.cis.umn.edu:11119/77?ESL)
Short listings of ESL positions.

International Job Opportunities
(http://www.cc.emory.edu/OIA/work_abroad.html)
List of teaching positions in various countries.

Job Listings in Academia
(http://volvo.gslis.utexas.edu/~acadres/jla.html)
A collection of Internet resources for the academic job hunter.

Key Resources for International Work
(http://www.umich.edu/~icenter/wrkbib94.htm)
Good info compiled by William Nolting from the University of Michigan International Center.

Miscellaneous ESL Employment Listings
(http://www.pvp.com/joblist.htm)
Employment listings from the ESL Virtual Catalog.

Search for ESL Jobs
(gopher://chronicle.merit.edu:70/11/.ads/.ads-by-search)
Searchable index for positions announced in *Academe This Week*.

TESL Job Opportunities—Linguistics Funland
(http://math.unr.edu/linguistics/tesljob.html)
Links, resources, and job announcements from Kristina Pfaff-Harris's Linguistics Funland.

Times Higher Education Supplement
(http://www.timeshigher.newsint.co.uk/)
Worldwide jobs from the U.K.'s weekly, highly respected, educational paper.

United States Information Agency English Language Programs Division
(http://www.usia.gov/education/engteaching/eal-ndx.htm)
Information about USIS posts in more than 140 countries, from the English Language Programs Division of the United States Information Agency.

US JOBNET
(http://www.usjobnet.com/)
Listing of mostly K–12 teaching positions.

Volterre-Fr Job Links
(http://www.wfi.fr/volterre/joblinks.html)
ESL/EFL job links, job books, and tips from France's Volterre-Fr.

Zoom Employment Opportunities
(http://www.clasalle.qc.ca/Emploisa.html)
Assortment of international job opportunities (including ESL) from ZOOM Placement de Personnel.

Hong Kong

Hong Kong Jobs
(http://www.hkjobs.com/)
A site dedicated to job openings in Hong Kong.

Indonesia

American Language Center of Jakarta
(http://www.indo.net.id/ALC/ALC.HTM)
Some information about teaching in Indonesia, from the American Language Center of Jakarta.

Information

Bibliography for International Job Opportunities
(http://www.adm.uwaterloo.ca/infocecs/CRC/publications/abroad/abroad.add.resources.html)
Good bibliography from the University of Waterloo's Career Services.

ESL Jobs: Discussion
(http://www.pacificnet.net/~sperling/wwwboard3/wwwboard.html)
Interactive discussion board with lots of good information.

Information on Work Abroad
(http://www.istc.umn.edu)
Useful information from the International Study and Travel Center (ISTC).

IOP Best Bets for Teaching Abroad
(http://www.cie.uci.edu/~cie/iop/teaching.html)
Links and information from UC Irvine's International Opportunities program.

Overview to Work Abroad
(http://www.umich.edu/~icenter/overv94.htm)
Useful tips from the University of Michigan International Center.

Teaching Abroad Without a Certificate
(http://www.umich.edu/~icenter/tefl94ic.htm)
Little or no ESL/EFL training? Check out this article!

Work Abroad
(http://www.umich.edu/~icenter/teach.html)
The University of Michigan International Center's guide to teaching abroad.

Japan

AEON Corporation
(http://www.aeonet.com/)
Information about teaching for one of Japan's largest language schools.

Colleges and Universities in Japan
(http://www.mit.edu:8001/people/cdemello/jp.html)
Christina DeMello's up-to-date listing of colleges and universities in Japan.

Consulate General of Japan in San Francisco
(http://www.infojapan.com/cgjsf/index.htm)
You'll find plenty of useful facts about Japan, including teaching information.

JALT
(http://langue.hyper.chubu.ac.jp/jalt)
The home page of the Japan Association for Language Teaching.

Japan Exchange and Teaching Alumni Association
(http://www.jet.org)
JET resource from Michael McVey.

Ohayo Sensei
(http://math.unr.edu/linguistics/ohayo-sensei.html)
Updated twice monthly, this is probably the Internet's finest source of English teaching jobs in Japan.

Surviving in Japan
(http://www.st.rim.or.jp/~snash/Jsurvive.html)
Outstanding article from Scott Nash.

Teaching English in Japan: Guide to Getting a Job
(http://www.wizweb.com/~susan/mainpage.html)
Susan Crowell's excellent guide to working in Japan.

Teaching English / Working In Japan
(http://www.infojapan.com/cgjsf/teaching.htm)
Advice from the Japan Information Center.

Teaching in Japan
(http://www.u-net.com/eflweb/japan0.htm)
An article written by John St. Paul, an English teacher who went unqualified to Japan to find a teaching job.

The Tokyo Journal
(http://japan.co.jp/tj/)
Online version of Tokyo's premier English language magazine.

Job Interview

The Briefcase Virtual Interview
(http://student.studentcenter.com/brief/virtual/virtual.htm)
The Virtual Interview contains actual interview questions ranging from "puff ball to killer."

Hot Seat
(http://www.kaplan.com/career/hotseat/)
Choose the best answer in this mock interview from Kaplan.

15 Popular Questions to Expect in an Interview
(http:// www.cacee.com/workweb/15questions.html)
Common interview questions from Ingenia Communications Corporation.

K-12 Overseas

International Schools in Japan
(http://www.SFBayArea.com/isij/)
A growing list of international schools in Japan.

International WWW School Registry
(http://web66.coled.umn.edu/schools.html)
Home pages of schools from around the world.

TIPS
(http://www.iteachnet.com/)
You'll find services and links for overseas teaching and living, a Web magazine for international school teachers and administrators, and a gallery of international schools.

Work Abroad
(http://www.umich.edu/~icenter/teach.html)
K–12 info from the University of Michigan's International Center.

Korea

Better Resource Homepage
(http://www.eslkorea.com)
ESL/EFL teacher recruiting organization, located in California.

Colleges and Universities in Korea
(http://www.mit.edu:8001/people/cdemello/kr.html)
Christina DeMello's list of colleges and universities in Korea.

English Teacher Positions in Korea
(http://www.ncmc.cc.mi.us:443/esl/jobs.html)
Listings of teaching jobs in Korea.

Korean Connection
(http://soback.kornet.nm.kr/~wiegand)
Plenty of good info about living and working in Korea.

Korean Connection's Jobs
(http://soback.kornet.nm.kr/~wiegand/2jobs.htm)
The Korean Connection's listing of jobs. Updated weekly.

Korea Herald Home Page
(http://www.koreaherald.co.kr)
Daily English news from Korea.

Korea-Net Positions
(http://www.asia-net.com/korea-net.html)
Positions in a variety of fields.

Teach English in South Korea
(http://www.interchg.ubc.ca/dsung/)
Based in Vancouver, Canada, Lim's Services Group recruits English language instructors for South Korea.

Teaching English in Korean Hakwons
(http://www.well.com/user/greg/)
Information on Korean Hakwons, which are privately owned extracurricular schools.

Teaching in Korea
(http://www.ecrknox.com/korea/teach.htm)
Home page of Melanie Graham's teacher recruitment company.

Teach Korea
(http://home.aol.com/Teachkorea)
Recruits EFL teachers for South Korea.

Latin America

Positions in Latin America
(http://www.umich.edu/~icenter/tefl94ic.htm#Latin)
Some information from William Nolting and Jeannine Lorenger.

Middle East

Faculty of Medicine of Kuwait University
(http://hsccwww.kuniv.edu.kw/fom/dept/ENGLISH/TeachatKU.html)
Teaching positions at the English Language Division of the Faculty of Medicine of Kuwait University.

Kuwait University Job Vacancies
(http://www.kuniv.edu.kw/ku_vacancies.html)
Job openings in Kuwait, presented to you by Kuwait University Computer Services.

The Leslie Corporation
(http://www.nettap.com/~tlc/)
Employment opportunities and information on several countries in the Middle East.

SASIS Middle East Employment Recruiter
(http://www.sasis.com/)
Several teaching positions in the Middle East.

Miscellaneous

Career Path
(http://www.careerpath.com/)
Employment classifieds from 21 U.S. newspapers.

E-Span CareerPro Database
(http://espan2.espan.com/cgi-bin/gate2?espan~simple/index.html)
Search E-Span's employment listings database.

Internet Job Surfer
(http://www.rpi.edu/dept/cdc/jobsurfer/)
List of commercial organizations providing either job databases, resume listings, or other services for Human Resources.

OCC Jobs
(http://www.occ.com/occ/SearchAllJobs.html)
Help from the Online Career Center.

Resumé

EFL WEB'S Resumé and Curriculum Vitae Page
(http://www.u-net.com/eflweb/resume.htm)
Get your resumé online for free, compliments of EFLWEB.

ESL Jobs: Wanted
(http://www.pacificnet.net/~sperling/wwwboard5/wwwboard.html)
Add a mini-profile to an expanding teacher database.

Singapore

Job Opportunities in Singapore
(http://www.ofs.ac.sg/ofs/jobs.html)
Teaching opportunities at Singapore's Overseas Family School.

Taiwan

ALE Language School
(http://www.alenet.com.tw/
Home page of the Actual Living English Language School.

Colleges and Universities in Taiwan
(http://www.mit.edu:8001/people/cdemello/tw.html)
Cristina DeMello's listing of colleges and universities in Taiwan.

Hess Language Schools
(http://www.hess.com.tw)
Home page of Taiwan's largest children's English school.

Taipei Language Institute
(http://www.transend.com.tw/~tli/page.html)
Information about teaching English in Taiwan at the Taipei Language Institute.

Taiwan Cyberpedia
(http:///www.cybertaiwan.com)
An English language information resource for Taiwan, including a section on language resources for teachers.

Teaching English in Taiwan
(http://www.u-net.com/eflweb/taiwan0.htm)
Article written by Hall Houston, an English teacher who went to Taiwan in 1991.

Thailand

Bangkok Post Career Classifieds
(http://www.bangkokpost.net/classifieds/classindex.html)
Daily job postings from the Bangkok Post.

ECC Thailand
(http://www.eccthai.com/jobs.htm)
Job vacancies at 50 ECC locations in Thailand.

SiamJob
(http://www.siam.net/jobs/)
Job vacancies, a mailing list, and an online resume service.

Teaching in Thailand
(http://eslcafe.com/thailand/)
Article written by by Krittika Onsanit, an English teacher in Thailand from October 1991 to October 1992 .

Volunteer

International Organizations
(http://144.96.225.66/internorgs.html)
List of organizations that will assist in finding work abroad.

Peace Corps Home Page
(http://www.peacecorps.gov/)
Everything there is to know about becoming a Peace Corps volunteer.

Teach for America
(http://www.americanexpress.com/student/right/orgs/teach/teach.html)
Teach for America is the "national teacher corps of talented, dedicated, recent college graduates who commit two years to teach in urban and rural public schools."

Teach/Work Abroad Opportunities
(http://www.bc.edu/bc_org/avp/acavp/inprg/graduate/grad-work-abroad.html)
Advice from Boston College's Office of International Programs.

The USIA Fulbright Teacher Exchange
(http://www.usia.gov/education/fulbtex.htm)
Open to teachers and administrators from the elementary through the post-secondary levels.

Voluntary Service Overseas
(http://www.oneworld.org/vso/rio.html)
VSO has over 1,700 volunteers working in 57 developing countries.

WorldTeach
(http://www.hiid.harvard.edu/programs/wteach.htm)
Teaching in China, Costa Rica, Ecuador, Namibia, Poland, South Africa, and Thailand.

Copyright Law on the Net

> "*In order to avoid the rocky shoals of copyright infringement, the veteran net surfer is well served by an understanding of the basic tenets of copyright law.*"
>
> **Benedict O'Mahoney, Attorney**

Law in Cyberspace can be, to say the least, extremely vague and often frustrating to interpret, and this is especially true of copyright law. Not everyone agrees on this highly debated topic, and it may take a few lawsuits and Supreme Court decisions to understand things a little more clearly, but here are answers to some of the most common questions on how copyright law works in Cyberspace.

What is copyright law?

A copyright law usually gives a copyright owner the exclusive right to control copying of a writing, recording, picture, or electronic transcription.

Is it true that copyright law doesn't exist in Cyberspace?

Not true at all. In fact, just about everything you produce yourself on the Internet will be protected under copyright law, and that includes e-mail, USENET and mailing list postings, graphics, and Web pages.

How does one obtain copyright protection?

As soon as you have written your work—whether it's an e-mail message, posting to a newsgroup, or a Web creation—it's automatically copyrighted. You don't have to send it to the Library of Congress or even put a copyright notice on it.

But doesn't my Web page need one of those copyright symbols on it for copyright protection?

This was true in the past, but not now. Having the symbol on your page, however, may give you a little more protection because it makes the assertion that it is under copyright protection.

What's Public Domain?

Public Domain is material that, for whatever reason, is not protected by copyright law and can be used freely without permission. One example is a copyright that has expired.

Does copyright law mean that I cannot use another's work for inspiration?

No, you are welcome to use someone's creation for inspiration, but you are not allowed to copy it without permission. Remember, you cannot copyright ideas, facts, titles, names, or short phrases.

If someone posts a message to a discussion list, can I quote that person in my response?

The answer is *probably* yes. The message was copyrighted, but because it was posted onto a discussion list, the person gave an *implicit license* for others to quote.

Am I breaking the law by linking someone's home page to my home page?

This question is being debated all over the Net. As long as you don't try to take credit for the work, there doesn't seem to be a problem because, like a telephone number or street address, a URL is not copyrightable. In addition, by being on the Web, the person has given others *implied* permission to add a link to your Web page. You may not, however, use someone's actual list of links if that list demonstrates some originality.

Do I need to inform the Web site if I link their page to mine?

No, it's not mandatory, but it is good netiquette.

Is it legal to use images and graphics from the Web?

You can use the images if they are in the Public Domain. Otherwise, you must obtain permission from the copyright owner.

Can I post personal e-mail to a discussion list?

Probably not, because there was not an implicit license (besides, it's not very nice, is it?).

How about English language material on the Net. Can I copy it for my classes?

Well, that depends on whether the author made the material explicitly free to copy ("you are free to use this material"), or explicitly *not* free to copy ("this material is not to be copied!"). However in some cases, the right to copy is implicit (and this is where the law gets a little murky). You'll find, however, that there is a lot of excellent material on the Internet that is Public Domain and free for you to use.

Remember: You *can* copy: **Facts**
Ideas . . .
But *not* the **Words**

Since the law in Cyberspace is continuously evolving, here are some places to help you keep up-to-date with the latest developments.

Copyright Law Meets the World Wide Web
(http://www.acm.org/crossroads/xrds2-2/weblaw.html)
Informative 1995 article written by Matt Rosenberg.

The Copyright Website
(http://www.benedict.com/)
Created by attorney Benedict O'Mahoney, this is the best source of easy-to-understand info on copyright law.

Cyberspace Law for Non-Lawyers
(http://www.counsel.com/cyberspace/)
Online seminar presented by Prof. Larry Lessig, University of Chicago Law School, Prof. David Post, Georgetown University Law Center, Prof. Eugene Volokh, UCLA School of Law, and the Cyberspace Law Institute and Counsel Connect, the online community for lawyers.

10 Big Myths About Copyright Explained
(http://www.clari.net/brad/copymyths.html)
Brad Templeton's answers to common myths about copyright on the Net.

U.S. Copyright Office
(http://lcweb.loc.gov/copyright/)
Help from the Library of Congress.

Web Law FAQ
(http://www.patents.com/weblaw.sht)
Frequently Asked Questions from the law firm of Oppedahl & Larson.

Appendix A: Country Codes

Wonder where an e-mail message is from? Here is a complete list of countries, alphebetized by country code:

AD	Andorra
AE	United Arab Emirates
AF	Afghanistan
AG	Antigua and Barbuda
AI	Anguilla
AL	Albania
AM	Armenia
AN	Netherlands Antilles
AO	Angola
AQ	Antarctica
AR	Argentina
AS	American Samoa
AT	Austria
AU	Australia
AW	Aruba
AZ	Azerbaijan
BA	Bosnia and Herzegovina
BB	Barbados
BD	Bangladesh
BE	Belgium
BF	Burkina Faso
BG	Bulgaria
BH	Bahrain
BI	Burundi
BJ	Benin
BM	Bermuda
BN	Brunei
BO	Bolivia
BR	Brazil
BS	Bahamas
BT	Bhutan
BV	Bouvet Island
BW	Botswana
BY	Belarus
BZ	Belize
CA	Canada
CC	Cocos (Keeling) Islands
CF	Central African Republic
CG	Congo
CH	Switzerland
CI	Cote D'Ivoire (Ivory Coast)
CK	Cook Islands
CL	Chile
CM	Cameroon
CN	China
CO	Colombia
CR	Costa Rica
CS	Czechoslovakia (former)
CU	Cuba
CV	Cape Verde
CX	Christmas Island
CY	Cyprus
CZ	Czech Republic
DE	Germany
DJ	Djibouti
DK	Denmark
DM	Dominica
DO	Dominican Republic

DZ	Algeria	HN	Honduras
EC	Ecuador	HR	Croatia (Hrvatska)
EE	Estonia	HT	Haiti
EG	Egypt	HU	Hungary
EH	Western Sahara	ID	Indonesia
ER	Eritrea	IE	Ireland
ES	Spain	IL	Israel
ET	Ethiopia	IN	India
FI	Finland	IO	British Indian Ocean Territory
FJ	Fiji	IQ	Iraq
FK	Falkland Islands (Malvinas)	IR	Iran
FM	Micronesia	IS	Iceland
FO	Faroe Islands	IT	Italy
FR	France	JM	Jamaica
FX	France, Metropolitan	JO	Jordan
GA	Gabon	JP	Japan
GB	Great Britain (UK)	KE	Kenya
GD	Grenada	KG	Kyrgyzstan
GE	Georgia	KH	Cambodia
GF	French Guiana	KI	Kiribati
GH	Ghana	KM	Comoros
GI	Gibraltar	KN	Saint Kitts and Nevis
GL	Greenland	KP	Korea (North)
GM	Gambia	KR	Korea (South)
GN	Guinea	KW	Kuwait
GP	Guadeloupe	KY	Cayman Islands
GQ	Equatorial Guinea	KZ	Kazakhstan
GR	Greece	LA	Laos
GS	S. Georgia and S. Sandwich Isls.	LB	Lebanon
GT	Guatemala	LC	Saint Lucia
GU	Guam	LI	Liechtenstein
GW	Guinea-Bissau	LK	Sri Lanka
GY	Guyana	LR	Liberia
HK	Hong Kong	LS	Lesotho
HM	Heard and McDonald Islands	LT	Lithuania

LU	Luxembourg
LV	Latvia
LY	Libya
MA	Morocco
MC	Monaco
MD	Moldova
MG	Madagascar
MH	Marshall Islands
MK	Macedonia
ML	Mali
MM	Myanmar
MN	Mongolia
MO	Macau
MP	Northern Mariana Islands
MQ	Martinique
MR	Mauritania
MS	Montserrat
MT	Malta
MU	Mauritius
MV	Maldives
MW	Malawi
MX	Mexico
MY	Malaysia
MZ	Mozambique
NA	Namibia
NC	New Caledonia
NE	Niger
NF	Norfolk Island
NG	Nigeria
NI	Nicaragua
NL	Netherlands
NO	Norway
NP	Nepal
NR	Nauru
NT	Neutral Zone
NU	Niue
NZ	New Zealand (Aotearoa)
OM	Oman
PA	Panama
PE	Peru
PF	French Polynesia
PG	Papua New Guinea
PH	Philippines
PK	Pakistan
PL	Poland
PM	St. Pierre and Miquelon
PN	Pitcairn
PR	Puerto Rico
PT	Portugal
PW	Palau
PY	Paraguay
QA	Qatar
RE	Reunion
RO	Romania
RU	Russian Federation
RW	Rwanda
SA	Saudi Arabia
SB	Solomon Islands
SC	Seychelles
SD	Sudan
SE	Sweden
SG	Singapore
SH	St. Helena
SI	Slovenia
SJ	Svalbard and Jan Mayen Islands
SK	Slovak Republic
SL	Sierra Leone
SM	San Marino
SN	Senegal
SO	Somalia

SR	Suriname
ST	Sao Tome and Principe
SU	USSR (former)
SV	El Salvador
SY	Syria
SZ	Swaziland
TC	Turks and Caicos Islands
TD	Chad
TF	French Southern Territories
TG	Togo
TH	Thailand
TJ	Tajikistan
TK	Tokelau
TM	Turkmenistan
TN	Tunisia
TO	Tonga
TP	East Timor
TR	Turkey
TT	Trinidad and Tobago
TV	Tuvalu
TW	Taiwan
TZ	Tanzania
UA	Ukraine
UG	Uganda
UK	United Kingdom
UM	U.S. Minor Outlying Islands
US	United States
UY	Uruguay
UZ	Uzbekistan
VA	Vatican City State (Holy See)
VC	Saint Vincent and the Grenadines
VE	Venezuela
VG	Virgin Islands (British)
VI	Virgin Islands (U.S.)
VN	Vietnam
VU	Vanuatu
WF	Wallis and Futuna Islands
WS	Samoa
YE	Yemen
YT	Mayotte
YU	Yugoslavia
ZA	South Africa
ZM	Zambia
ZR	Zaire
ZW	Zimbabwe
COM	U.S. Commercial
EDU	U.S. Educational
GOV	U.S. Government
INT	International
MIL	U.S. Military
NET	Network
ORG	Nonprofit organization
ARPA	Old style Arpanet
NATO	NATO field

Appendix B: Error Messages

Most of the time you'll find that surfing the Web is a fairly hassle-free experience, but there might be moments of frustration, such as when you try to enter a Web site and instead receive odd error messages. Don't panic! Here are explanations to some of the most common Netscape error messages.

`400 - Bad request`

Meaning: The URL is probably wrong. Try checking the URL again, especially uppercase and lowercase letters, colons, and slashes.

`401 - Unauthorized`

Meaning: You're trying to get into a page to which you don't have access, or else you're using an incorrect password. If you do have access, try again.

`403 - Forbidden`

Meaning: You don't have access to the document. Not much can be done about this, but you could try again later.

`404 - Not found`

Meaning: Either the address is incorrect, or the page no longer exists. Try typing the address again.

`503 - Service unavailable`

Meaning: The Web site is probably down. Try the address again later.

`Bad file request`

Meaning: The form is not compatible with your browser. Try e-mailing to the site's *Webmaster*, or else try the address again with another Web browser.

`Failed DNS lookup`

Meaning: The Domain Name Server can't translate the URL to a valid Internet address. This is most likely because of an incorrect URL, but it could also mean that the Web site is having technical problems. Type the URL carefully, and try again.

`NNTP server error`

Meaning: This means that you can't access a particular USENET newsgroup. Be sure that the URL is correct, and, if you still have problems, try again later.

`File contains no data`

Meaning: The page appears empty because there isn't a Web page document on it. It's possible that the document is being updated just as you tried to access it, and only appears empty. Try again later.

`Host unavailable`

Meaning: The site you are trying to access is probably down for maintenance. Try again later.

`Connection refused by host`

Meaning: You are not allowed to access this document. However, If you think that you do have access, try contacting the site's Webmaster (the person that maintains the Web site).

`Unable to locate the server`

Meaning: The URL is incorrect, or the server doesn't exist. What can be done about it? Be sure that you have the correct address.

`Network connection was refused by the server`

Meaning: The server is probably busy. Try again later.

`Too many users`

Meaning: Too many users are attempting to access the site. Try again later.

`Unable to locate host`

Meaning: The Web site might be down for maintenance, or the connection may have been lost. Try clicking the Reload button, or try again later.

Appendix C: Netspeak

An entire new way of communicating is evolving on the Net and, like it or not, your students are going to pick up some of this new way of "speaking." Need an *addy*? Are you feeling @%&$%&? Is the other teacher *afk*? See below for a translation!

Slang

@%&$%& = bad word!
addy = address
adn = any day now
afaik = as far as I know
afk = away from keyboard
aol = America Online
atta = at a
b4 = before
bak = back at keyboard
bbye = bye bye
bcnu = be seeing you
bo = back off
brb = be right back
btw = by the way
bux = bucks
chk = check
cu = see you
cummunicate = communicate
cyber- = a prefix that makes a word computer related.
Cyberspace = a term for the Internet
da = the
diik = darned if I know
enuf = enough
<evil g> = evil grin
fitb = fill in the blank
flame = fighting with words on the Internet
foaf = friend of a friend
fone = phone
fotfl = falling on the floor laughing
ftbomh = from the bottom of my heart
fwiw = for what it's worth
fya = for your amusement
fyi = for your information
<g> = grin
graphix = graphics
ga = go ahead
giwist = gee, I wish I said that
hand = have a nice day
hewwo = hello?
hhok = ha ha, only kidding
hth = hit the hay (go to sleep)
huggle = hug
idk = I don't know
imo = in my opinion
iow = in other words
k... = okay
kewl = cool
kutgw = keep up the good work
l8tr = later
laff = laugh
laffin = laughing
laffs = laughs
lag = a slow period of data transfer
link = way to transfer from one site to another
llap = live long and prosper
lma = last minute addition
lol = laughing out loud
lurker = someone who only reads and doesn't post to a group
member = remember
myob = mind your own business
narf = cool
nawt = not!

net potato = someone who spends a great deal of time surfing the net
newbie = a new user of the Internet
nuttin = nothing
o&o = over & out
oic = oh I see
otoh = on the other hand
pov = point of view
ppl = people
puter = computer
real world = a person's life outside of the Internet
rite = right
rotfl = rolling on the floor laughing
rsn = real soon now
sbi = so be it
sherlock = someone who can find almost anything on the Internet
sig = short for signature
site = an Internet address or a place on the Internet
skool = school
smax = smacks
smiley = used to show emotions
snail mail = postal mail
sohf = sense of humor failure
some1 = someone
sri = sorry
st00pid = stupid
sulx = sulks
summin = something
surfing the net = the act of exploring the World Wide Web
tafn = that's all for now
tbc = to be continued
thanx = thanks
thru = through
tia = thanks in advance
tks = thanks
tnx = thanks
tru = true
ttul = talk to you later
u = you
ur = you are
<vbg> = very big grin
w8 = wait
wayz = ways
whirrled = world
wif = with
wysiwyg = what you see is what you get
ywia = you're welcome in advance

Smileys

Since most communication on the Net is done with text (though this is changing fast), you can't see the other person's body language and facial expressions, or hear the speech intonation. Needless to say, it's easy to create major misunderstandings! Don't fret: **Smileys**, also called **Emoticons**, can save the day.

:-) smile
:-] bigger smile
:-(frown
:-[bigger frown
|-) sleeping
{:-) toupee
:-{ really sad
;-) wink
:-D laughter
[] hugs
:•) happy clown
:•(sad clown

:-! smiley with pimple
:-$ smiley with braces
+-:-) priest
:-\ unsure smiley
:-/ lefty unsure smiley
:-< real sad smiley
:-x my lips are sealed
:-c bummed smiley
:-I Hmm?
:-{) mustache
:-& tongue tied

:-)> smiley with a goatee
:-)== smiley with a beard
:-)x smiley with a bow tie
};-> devilish wink
<:-) dumb question
=:-o Eeeeeeek!
:-o Oh no!
:~(user is crying
:-~) user has a cold

Other Conventions

Emphasis

Asterisks are placed around a word or phrase for emphasis, as in the following example:

```
The ESL Cafe is the *best*
place on the Net!
```

Underscore

Underscores are added before and after text that would normally be underlined, as in:

```
_War and Peace_
```

Selected Bibliography

Here is a list of Internet books, categorized by topic. If you want a more detailed listing, head over to Kevin Savetz's truly amazing **The Un-official Internet Book List** (`http://redwood.northcoast.com/savetz/booklist/`), which has descriptions and information on hundreds of Internet-related books.

America Online

- Bowen, Charles. 1995. *The Hitchhiker's Guide to America Online*. New York: MIS Press.
- Price, Jonathan. 1995. *The Trail Guide to America Online*. Reading, Massachusetts: Addison Wesley.

Child Safety

- Carlson, Matt. *Childproof Internet: A Parent's Guide to Safe and Secure Online Access*. New York: MIS Press.
- Giagnocavo, Gregory, and Tim McLain. 1996. *Child Safety on the Internet*. Upper Saddle River, New Jersey: Prentice Hall.

CompuServe

- Beatty, Grace, David Gardner, and David Sauer. *Cruising CompuServe*. Rocklin, California: Prima Publishing.
- Tatters, Wes. 1995. *Navigating the Internet with CompuServe*. Indianapolis, Indiana: Sams.Net.

Connections

- Gilster, Paul. 1995. *The SLIP/PPP Connection*. New York: Wiley.

Dictionaries

- Crumlish, Christian. 1995. *The Internet Dictionary*. Alameda, California: SYBEX.
- Morse, David. 1996. *Cyber Dictionary*. Santa Monica, California: Knowledge Exchange.

Directories (Education)

- Minnesota/South Dakota Regional Adult Literacy Resource Center. 1995. *Internet Directory of Literacy and Adult Education Resources*. St. Paul, Minnesota: Minnesota/South Dakota Regional Adult Literacy Resource Center.
- Place, Ron. 1996. *Educator's Internet Yellow Pages*. Upper Saddle River, New Jersey: Prentice Hall PTR; Prentice-Hall International.
- Sharp, F. Vicki, G. Martin Levine, and M. Richard Sharp. 1996. *The Best Web Sites for Teachers*. Eugene, Oregon: ISTE.

Directories (General)

- Filo, David, and Jerry Yang. 1995. *Yahoo! Unluged*. Foster City, California: IDG Books Worldwide.
- Hahn, Harley. 1996. *The Internet Yellow Pages*. Berkeley, California: Osborne McGraw Hill.

E-mail

- Irvine, Mark. 1996. *Write Around the World.* Florence, Italy: Reporter Publications.
- Levine, John R. 1996. *Internet E-mail for Dummies.* Foster City, California: IDG Books Worldwide.
- Schneider, Bruce. 1995. *E-mail Security.* New York: John Wiley & Sons.
- Warschauer, Mark. 1995. *E-mail for English Teaching: Bringing the Internet and Computer Learning Networks Into the Language Classroom.* Alexandria, Virginia: Teachers of English to Speakers of Other Languages.

FAQs

- Young, Margaret Levine. 1995. *Internet FAQs.* Foster City, California: IDG Books Worldwide.

Genealogy

- Crowe, Elizabeth Powell. 1995. *Genealogy Online: Researching your Roots.* Blue Ridge Summit, Pennsylvania: Windcrest/McGraw-Hill.
- Eastman, Richard. 1995. *Your Roots: Total Genealogy Planning on your Computer.* Emeryville, California: 2D Press.

Emoticons

- Sanderson, David. 1993. *Smileys.* Sebastopol, California: O'Reilly & Associates.
- Tamosaitis, Nancy. 1994. *Net Talk.* Emeryville, California: Ziff-Davis Press.

Files

- Kientzle, Tim. 1995. *Internet File Formats.* Scottsdale, Arizona: Coriolis Group Books.

HTML

- Aronson, Larry. 1996. *HTML 3 Manual of Style.* Emeryville, California: 2D Press.
- Edtittel, Steve James. 1996. *HTML for Dummies.* Foster City, California: IDG Books Worldwide.
- Scharf, Dean. 1996. *HTML Quick Reference.* Indianapolis, Indiana: Que.

Internet (General)

- Gilster, Paul. 1995. *The New Internet Navigator.* New York: John Wiley & Sons.
- Hahn, Harley. 1996. *The Internet Complete Reference.* Berkeley, California: Osborne McGraw Hill.

Internet Relay Chat (IRC)

- Harris, Stuart. 1995. *The IRC Survival Guide.* New York: Addison-Wesley.
- Pyra, Marianne. 1995. *Using Internet Relay Chat.* Indianapolis, Indiana: Que.
- Rose, Donald. 1995. *Internet Chat Quick Tour.* Chapel Hill, North Carolina: Ventana.
- Toyer, Kathryn. 1996. *Learn Internet Relay Chat.* Plano, Texas: Wordware Publications.

ISDN

- Bryce, James. 1995. *Using ISDN.* Indianapolis, Indiana: Que.

Java

- Lemay, Laura, and Charles Perkins. 1996. *Teach Yourself Java in 21 Days.* Indianapolis, Indiana: Sams.Net.
- Walsh, Aaron. 1996. *Java for Dummies.* Foster City, California: IDG Books Worldwide.

Job Hunting

- Bounos, Shannon, and Arthur Karl. 1996. *How to Get Your Dream Job Using the Internet.* Scottsdale, Arizona: Coriolis Group Books.
- Kennedy, Joyce. 1995. *Hook Up, Get Wired!* New York: John Wiley & Sons.

Kids

- Pederson, Ted, and Francis Moss. 1995. *Internet for Kids.* Los Angeles: Price Stern Sloan.
- Polly, Jean Armous. 1996. *The Internet Kid's Yellow Pages.* Berkeley, California: Osborne McGraw Hill.

Law

- Cavazos, Edward, and Gavino Morin. 1995. *Cyberspace and the Law.* Cambridge, Massachusetts: The MIT Press.
- Evans, James. 1995. *Law on the Net.* Berkeley, California: Nolo Press.
- Rose, Lance. 1995. *Netlaw.* Berkeley, California: Osborne McGraw-Hill.

Modems

- Rathbone, Tina. 1996. *Modems for Dummies.* Foster City, California: IDG Books Worldwide.

Netscape

- Lemay, Laura, and Ned Snell. 1996. *Netscape Navigator Gold 3.* Indianapolis, Indiana: Sams.Net.
- Oliphant, Zan. 1996. *Netscape Plug-ins.* Indianapolis, Indiana: Sams.Net.
- Reichard, Kevin. 1996. *Teach Yourself Netscape Navigator 2.* New York: MIS Press.

Netiquette

- Mandel, Thomas, and Gerard Van Der Leun. 1996. *Rules of the Net.* New York: Hyperion.
- Rose, Donald. 1995. *Minding Your Cybermanners on the Internet.* Indianapolis, Indiana: Que.
- Shea, Virginia. 1994. *Netiquette.* San Francisco, California: Albion Books.

Parents

- Strudwick, Karen, John Spilket, and Jay Arney. 1995. *Internet for Parents.* Bellevue, Washington: Resolution Business Press.

Prodigy

- Johnson, Ned. 1995. *Navigating the Internet with Prodigy.* Indianapolis, Indiana: Sams.Net.
- Venditto, Gus. 1995. *Prodigy for Dummies.* Foster City, California: IDG Books Worldwide.

Projects

- Warschauer, Mark. 1995. *Virtual Connections : Online Activities and Projects for Networking Language Learners.* Manoa, Hawai'i: Second Language Teaching & Curriculum Center, Univ. of Hawaii at Manoa.

Research and Searches

- Gilster, Paul. 1996. *Finding It on the Internet: The Internet Navigator's Guide to Search Tools and Techniques.* New York: John Wiley & Sons.
- Rowland, Robin, and Dave Kinnaman. 1995. *Researching on the Internet.* Rocklin, California: Prima Publishing.

Searching the Web

- Hill, Brad. 1996. *World Wide Web Searching for Dummies.* Foster City, California: IDG Books Worldwide.

Students

- Clark, David. 1996. *Student's Guide to the Internet.* Indianapolis, Indiana: Que.
- Campbell, Dave and Mary Campbell. 1995. *The Student Guide to Doing Research on the Internet.* Reading, Massachusetts: Addison-Wesley.
- Corrigan, Dan. 1996. *The Internet University: College Courses by Computer.* Harwich, Massachusetts: Cape Software.
- Wolff, Michael. 1996. *Netstudy: Your Guide to Getting Better Grades.* New York: Wolff New Media.

Teachers

- Educational Research Service. 1996. *The Internet Roadmap for Educators.* Arlington, Virginia: Educational Research Service.
- Ellsworth, Jill. 1994. *Education on the Internet.* Indianapolis, Indiana: Sams.Net.
- Heide, Ann Linda Stilborne. 1996. *The Teacher's Complete and Easy Guide to the Internet.* Toronto: Trifolium Books.
- Serim, Ferdi. 1996. *NetLearning: Why Teachers Use the Internet.* Sebastopol, California: Songline Studios and O'Reilly & Assoc.
- Steen, Douglas, Mark Roddy, Derek Sheffield, Michael Bryan Stout, D.J. Hura. 1995. *Teaching with the Internet.* Bellevue, Washington: Resolution Busines Press.
- Williams, Bard. 1995. *The Internet for Teachers.* Foster City, California: IDG Books Worldwide.

Telephony

- Pulver, Jeff. 1996. *Internet Telephone Toolkit.* New York: Wiley Computer Publishing.
- Shapiro, Jeffrey R. 1996. *Computer Telephony Strategies.* Foster City, California: IDG Books Worldwide.

UNIX

- Reichard, Kevin, and Eric Johnson. 1994. *UNIX in Plain English.* New York: MIS Press.

USENET

- Mamer, Karl. 1996. *Get the News on USENET.* San Francisco, California: Motion Works Publications.
- Pfaffenberger, Bryan. 1995.*The USENET Book.* Reading, Massachusetts: Addison-Wesley.

Videoconferencing

- Rustici, Robert. 1995. *Enhanced CU-SeeMe.* New York: MIS Press.

Glossary of Internet Terms

ASCII

American Standard Code for Information Interchange. Plain, basic text that can be read by all computers.

attachment

The ability to include files, graphics, and software with your e-mail.

bandwidth

The range of how much data can be transferred by a line at one time. A larger bandwidth means that more information can travel on the network at one time.

baud

The speed at which a modem can transfer data.

Bcc

Blind Carbon Copy. E-mail message sent to several different people, whose identity is kept secret from the primary recipient.

binary file

A type of file that contains something other than plain text, such as formatted text, pictures, sound, software, and video.

binHex

A method of converting Macintosh binary files (such as graphics and software) into ASCII text.

body

The message area of an e-mail message.

bookmark

A marker that enables you to return to a Web page again on a later date.

bounced message

E-mail that is returned when, for whatever reason, it cannot reach its destination in Cyberspace.

bps

Bits per second. Speed, measured in bits, at which a modem transfers data.

browser

See **Web browser**.

cache

Pronounced "cash." The area of your computer's hard drive that temporarily stores a Web page's text and graphics so that the page loads quickly on your next visit.

Cc

Carbon Copy. A method whereby you can send the same letter to several different people.

Chat

A way of communicating in real time with other Internet users, usually by typing the words at your computer keyboard.

commercial service

One of the large online services, such as America Online, CompuServe, and Prodigy.

compressed file

A file that is condensed in order to take up less space. Many files on the Internet are compressed and require special software to be decompressed.

counter

A Web page addition that keeps track of how many visitors have "hit" your page.

Cu-SeeMe

One of the most popular videoconferencing software, developed by Cornell University.

Cyberspace

A popular term for the Internet.

dedicated line

A high-speed phone line that directly transfers information from your computer to the rest of the Internet.

demo software

Software that you can download and try before you buy.

dial-up connection

A connection to the Internet via your modem.

DNS

Domain Name Server. A machine service that finds the exact location of a URL.

Domain Name

The name of the host computer that is directly connected to the Internet.

dot

The word used instead of "period" when talking about an Internet address. For example, "`My home page is eslcafe dot com.`"

download

To transfer a file from one computer to another computer, usually via a modem.

e-mail

Electronic mail, that is, messages sent over the Internet.

Emoticon

See **Smiley**.

Eudora

A popular graphical e-mail program for Macintosh and Windows, used with a direct or SLIP/PPP connection.

FAQs

Frequently Asked Questions. These files are found all over the Internet and are a great way to learn about a new subject.

FTP

File Transfer Protocol. A method for transferring files over the Internet.

Finger

A program used to find information about another Internet user.

flame

To angrily and unreasonably attack another person over the Internet.

followup

A response to a posted message, usually in a newsgroup.

Freenet

A community-based network that furnishes free or inexpensive access to the Internet.

freeware

Software that you can download and use for free.

GIF

Graphical Interchange Format. A format, developed by CompuServe, that is the most common way to store pictures on the Internet.

gopher

A menu-driven guide to Internet directories, organized by subject.

gopherspace

The part of the Internet to which a gopher program can go.

graphics

Pictures and images found on the Internet.

helper application

A program that helps your Web browser view a file that it cannot recognize, such as animation and video.

hits

A request to the Web server to send a particular file. When you enter my home page, for example, you have made one "hit."

home page

The main Web page of an individual, group, or organization.

hotlist

A person's bookmarks.

host

The computer that is directly connected to the Internet.

HQX

Suffix for a binHex file, a popular format for transferring Macintosh binary files over the Internet.

HTML

HyperText Markup Language. The language used to create documents on the World Wide Web.

hyperlink

Clickable text on the World Wide Web that will transport you to another Web page.

hypertext

Most commonly found on the World Wide Web, this is a style of text where users can click on a hyperlink and be transported to another Web page.

Internet

The largest interconnected network of computers in the world.

Internet Service Provider (ISP)

An organization or company that offers access to the Internet.

IP address

A unique address for a computer on the Internet.

IRC

Internet Relay Chat. A popular program that allows real-time chatting with people anywhere in the world.

ISDN

Integrated Services Digital Network. High-speed digital telephone access to the Internet.

Java

A programming language from Sun Microsystems that allows users to run a variety of programs on the World Wide Web.

key pals

Pen pals that communicate via e-mail.

link

See **hyperlink**.

List Address

The address where you send a message to everyone subscribed to a patricular mailing list.

List Server Address

The address where you send commands (i.e. `subscribe` and `unsubscribe`) to a particular mailing list.

listproc

Increasingly popular mailing list program.

listserv

The most common mailing list program, which automatically sends and receives e-mail to and from a subscribed group of people.

lurkers

Readers of newsgroup or mailing list messages who never post.

Lynx

A popular text-based Web browser.

Machine Address

The address to which you send an e-mail message. For example, `eslcafe.com`, is my machine address.

mailing list

Group discussion conducted via e-mail.

majordomo

A common mailing list program found on the Internet.

Microsoft Explorer

One of the most popular Web browsers around, compliments of Mr. Gates.

mirror site

A site that replicates the contents of another site.

modem

Modulator-demodulator. A device that links one computer to another over standard telephone lines.

MOO

MUD Object Oriented. A virtual environment where people can "talk" to each other in virtual "rooms."

MUD

Multiuser dimension or multiuser dungeon. A role-playing game in which players use commands to navigate, chat, solve puzzles, and even fight monsters.

the Net

Common term for the Internet.

Netiquette

Good manners on the Internet.

Netizen

Members of the Internet community.

Netscape

One of the most popular Web browsers in the world.

Neteach-L

One of the very best mailing lists for ESL/EFL teachers.

Newbie

A beginning Internet user.

Newsgroups

USENET message areas where you can discuss almost any topic imaginable.

Newsreader

The program that allows you to read USENET's newsgroups.

offline

The time that you are disconnected from the Internet (like, in the shower!).

online

The time you are connected to the Internet.

password

The secret code necessary to enter a computer system.

Pine

Popular UNIX e-mail program.

plug-in

A program that expands the capability of your Web browser. Popular plug-ins include Shockwave (for sound and video), Real Audio (for audio broadcasts), and MPEGplay (for video).

port number

A unique number that identifies a telnet address, often necessary to connect to certain MOOs.

POP

Post Office Protocol. The mail server that distributes your incoming and outgoing e-mail.

PPP

Point-to-Point Protocol. One of the ways that you can enjoy browsing the Web over a phone line.

Public Domain

Material that, for whatever reason, is not protected by copyright law and can be used freely without permission.

Real Audio

A popular plug-in that allows you to receive live audio over the Internet.

real time

The Internet term for something live, such as Internet Relay Chat (IRC).

schMooze University

A MOO for English learning and discussion.

search engine

Powerful Internet tool that helps you find what you're looking for.

shocked

Term applied to Web pages when they are running Macromedia's Shockwave, which offers interactive animation and sound.

server

A computer that provides a certain service, such as e-mail, gopher, or the World Wide Web.

shareware

Free software that can be downloaded, but for which payment is voluntary.

shell account

The most basic, text-only access to the Internet, usually through UNIX.

signature

A text file at the end of an e-mail message or newsgroup posting, usually containing personal information. Sometimes called *SIG*.

site

The actual location of a computer.

SLIP

Serial Line Internet Protocol. Like PPP, SLIP provides a method for browsing the Web over a phone line.

Smiley

Text used to imply emotion and humor in Internet messages. Also called **emoticon**.

SMTP

Simple Mail Transfer Protocol. The language that your mail server uses to send and receive e-mail on the Internet.

snail mail

Mail delivered the old-fashioned way, before the existence of e-mail!

Source Code

The actual HTML of a Web page.

SPAM

Sending Particularly Annoying Messages. A term for sending out a single message to multiple mailing lists or newsgroups (such as "Make Money Fast"). It's despised and very bad netiquette.

surfing

Slang for spending time on the Net.

Sysop

System Operator. The person who manages an Internet site.

tag

The HTML codes used to designate the style of text, links, graphics, and other essentials.

TCP/IP

Transmission Control Protocol/ Internet Protocol. Standards that enable communication among all the various computers on the Internet, developed by the University of California for the Department of Defense.

telephony

Telephone-like communication over the Internet.

telnet

A program that allows you to log in to any computer on the Internet, anywhere in the world.

TESL

Teaching English as a Second Language

TESL-L

The largest and most comprehensive TESL mailing list.

TESOL

Teachers of English to Speakers of Other Languages, with over 18,000 members from 100 different countries.

thread

Replies to a particular newsgroup message.

TIA

The Internet Adapter. A device that enables you to emulate a SLIP/PPP connection on a basic terminal dial-up account.

TOEFL

Test of English as a Foreign Language

UNIX

A computer language, first developed by AT&T, used by many of the computers on the Internet.

Upload

To transfer a file from your local computer to a remote computer.

URL

Uniform Resource Locator, pronounced U-R-L. A World Wide Web address. For example, `http://www.eslcafe.com/` is the URL of my home page, the ESL Cafe.

USENET

A collection of thousands of newsgroups for exchanging messages on almost every imaginable topic.

User Name

The unique account name given to a user on a system. My user name, for example, is `sperling`.

Veronica

Very Easy Rodent-Oriented Netwide Index to Computerized Archives. A powerful search engine that enables you to search gopherspace for files and information.

virus

A damaging program that is transferred from one computer to another computer via phone lines or floppy disks. Virus scanning software can usually save the day.

VRML

Virtual Reality Modeling Language. Creates 3-D regions on the Web.

Web board

A way for people to easily read and post messages directly onto a Web page from their Web browser.

Web browser

A program that enables you to navigate and view the World Wide Web. Netscape and Microsoft Explorer are the most popular, but Lynx can also be used by those with a basic terminal connection.

Web master

The person who creates and maintains a Web site.

Web page

A document on the World Wide Web that can assimilate graphics, sounds, and video, and that links to other Web pages, FTP sites, gophers, and other Internet resources.

White Pages

A massive list of individual Internet users.

World Wide Web

Also called the Web and WWW, the World Wide Web is fast becoming the most popular area of the Internet. The Web allows you to easily traverse the Internet using hyperlinks to explore a variety of linked resources, including USENET newsgroups, FTP, telnet, and gopher sites.

WYSIWYG

What You See Is What You Get. A form of word processing in which the screen display (what you see) reflects the appearance of the printed page (what you get). Pronounced Wiszy-Whig.

Yahoo

One of the oldest and most popular search directories on the World Wide Web.

Zip

File-compression standard for DOS and Windows.

Index

C

E

F

G

M

N

Q

R

S

T

Y

Z